Right-Sizing Your Home

Right-Sizing Your Home

How To Make Your House Fit Your Lifestyle GALE C. STEVES

Northwest Arm Press

Acknowledgements

every book starts with an inspiration, then it blossoms and eventually becomes a reality. There are those who helped me in the planting of the idea, pulling the weeds as I wrote, and then worked on the harvest. First, my husband Philip Perrone, without whose support and understanding I might never have started writing this book—especially in the middle of the night when my best inspirations hit. And then there was Cricket, my Welsh terrier, who snuggled up next to me, keeping me company when I was writing in those wee hours. Plus, I owe a tremendous thanks to the following:

For the creative team of people behind me, who coddled, corrected, and cared: Mitch Shostak and Corey Kuepfer of Shostak Studios, Richard Balestrino, Merle Ann Parker, Robin Edward Bernstein, Jennifer Kervin, and Katherine Howlett. For John Driemen, Northwest Arm Press, who believed in Right-Sizing from the beginning. With their support and dedication, this book is even better than I imagined. They added immeasurably to this project in so many ways, and I could not have done it without their help.

For the friends and family who encouraged me from the sidelines: Roger Steves, Patty Broadley, Janet Schlesinger, Rhea Alexander and Dave Glassman, Edward Abramson and Susan Ludlow, Peggy Hamilton, Richard and Lesley Thorne, Anne Martin and Howard Schrott, Virginia Kennedy, Patricia Bowling, Mervyn Kaufman, Mary Witte, Patricia Bouley, Kay Degenhardt, Paul Thompson, and Ivan Saul Cutler.

And for the myriad of people who shared information and ideas with me over the years, patiently answered my questions, and were a powerful influence on my thinking: Connie Edwards, CKD, CBD; Paul Radoy; John Troxell, CMG; Florence Perchuk, CKD; Harold Martin; Wayne Susag; Sarah Reep, CKD, CBD; Howard Katz; Diana Schrage; Lynn Schrage; Lisa Lennard; Liz Sleeman; Lori Marrero, CPO; Barry J. Izsak, CPO, CRTS; Patricia Gaylor, CKD; Susan Serra, CKD; Laura Leist, CPO, CRTS; Jamie Goldberg, AKBD, CAPS; Steve Hodges, ASFD; Standolyn Robertson, CPO; Andrea Tobias; Paula Kendra; T.J. Gentle; Jack Lewis, ASFD; and Maude Bergeron.

Copyright© 2010 by Gale C. Steves

Published by Northwest Arm Press, Inc. Halifax, Nova Scotia • Designed by Corey Kuepfer, Shostak Studios Inc., New York, NY

Library and Archives Canada Cataloguing in Publication

Steves, Gale C., 1942-
Right-sizing your home : how to make your house fit your lifestyle / Gale C. Steves.

Includes index.
ISBN 978-1-926781-04-4

1. Dwellings--Remodeling. I. Title.

TH4816.S74 2010   643'.7   C2009-907192-4

10 9 8 7 6 5 4 3 2 1
First Edition

Printed in China

Right-Sizing

CONTENTS

Understand what Right-Sizing is all about, and you can immediately begin to make your house more livable. Learn the art of "RE"—rethink, revise, renew, and reuse the rooms in your home. Master the three tools you need to rediscover the space you have, now and in the future.

Review what you have, rethink what you need, and what you can do without. Discover what you can do to make your rooms work better, as well as what makes the best sense for the way you really live, with these five steps of Right-Sizing.

The kitchen is the hub of the house, but how efficient is it? How much storage do you need? How many people cook here? Make it work for you, not against you.

Where do you really eat? Out of pizza boxes on the coffee table? Revise your ideas about traditional dining and snacking spaces. Reinvent them to truly meet your lifestyle needs.

Relaxing takes place all over the house—from the family room to the bedroom. Make the most of your lounging space, whether you prefer cozy for two, or comfortable for a crowd.

Your Home

I Believe In Right-Sizing

It was in the late 1980s that I first noticed outsized homes around the country, with rooms that made no sense—either too big, too tall, or too small to be useful. At the same time, I realized that many older homes, some not so big, had rooms labeled with names that were no longer relevant to the way we live. What was wrong with this picture?

It seemed too many of us were squeezing our lives into spaces that didn't work for us, so we added on or bought bigger. Still, never noticing the root of the problem, parts of the house were ignored while others were over-used.

The big question was—and still is—how do you want to live? Forget preconceived notions of room function. Right-Sizing is the concept of working with what you have, by making better use of existing space. It's really all about space management; that is, assessing and managing the space within your home, and making it work—and work well—for you and your family.

Please read on, because I believe if you complete the exercises, and follow the advice in this book, you will be well on your way to living more comfortably in your Right-Sized home—now and for many years to come.

 Gale Steves

Live Better

No matter where you live, whether in a McMansion, a more modest home, or a townhouse, you are probably not living fully, or even well, in this space. If there are rooms that you only walk through or seldom use or you've begun to notice they don't meet your needs, then now is the time to Right-Size. This book is all about finding new ways to reinvent the space you have and to enjoy living better within it.

HOME STRETCH

This multipurpose room shows off the simple principle of Right-Sizing at its best. The flow from cooking and eating moves right into the relaxing area. It all works together.

What Is

Right-Sizing?

Right-Sizing is not downsizing. In fact, it is the opposite. You can live more fully in *your home if you Right-Size. No one wants to admit they are really cutting back, but whether you are driven by immediate or future needs, this is the time to shift gears.*

Right-Sizing Is Reinventing The Home

erhaps your house hasn't changed to keep up with your needs, and maybe you bought into the idea that what your real estate agent or builder told you was gospel truth. Do you really use your living room or dining room on a regular basis, even though the experts told you that you need to have them?

You or your spouse may be working from your home now, and working or not, everyone needs computer space. Your whole family may seldom sit down to eat together, because of various and busy schedules. Maybe your grown kids are planning to move back to the house. Your bathroom multifunctions. Forget about your guest room; who has time for guests, except on state occasions? And you use the couch as a crash pad after a long hard day. This is hardly the way you envisioned living in your house, but sadly, it's probably the reality.

Before you decide where you live doesn't work, and that you need to leave the neighborhood, read this book. It will help you repurpose each room of the house, to use the space you already have to achieve exactly what you want—a house with options, in terms of space and the way you really live! *That* is Right-Sizing

Some homes can be Right-Sized just so much before you need major help, and maybe more money than you are willing, or able, to spend. While I can't guarantee magic, I will assure you that you will look at your house with a new understanding and a different vision.

Right-Sizing Is Reimagining Your House

Right-Sizing Your Home is a self-help book that shows you how to "see" your house in a new way. This will aid you in assessing the space you have, and making it work better for you. There are unique worksheets to help you make important changes in the function, as well as the look of each individual room of your home. "Style Audits" in each chapter creatively evaluate your needs, so you can focus on the sections of the book that work best for your own individual requirements.

Right-Sizing Is Rethinking Your Existing Space

Just as the tools contained in each chapter will explain how to make better use of your residential space, you will also be in a better position to understand and accept your own day-to-day living needs. *Right-Sizing Your Home* provides ideas for creating step-by-step plans for improving your existing home, and even helps you think ahead to plan your future home.

Right-Sizing Is Reclaiming Your Rooms One-by-One

This book can be read from cover to cover. Yet it functions as a useful and creative guidebook to solving distinct, common living problems and situations. It is written in an interactive format, allowing you to find a specific solution without having to read the entire book.

From the moment you begin to browse the book, *Right-Sizing Your Home* will become an essential part of the reevaluation of your home. The style and structure make this the perfect personal guide for living better in the same space.

Remake One Room Into Another Using Right-Sizing Ideas

SHELF EXPRESSION
Your former laundry room has been easily converted into a craft area, and now you have an upstairs laundry, which is more convenient.

ORGANIZED LABOR
Or turn your craft room into a much needed laundry area with little or no effort, and the loss of one base cabinet. Use the workspace for folding and sorting clean clothes.

THE ART OF
"RE"

According to *Webster's Dictionary*, the prefix "re" means "return" or "back." When it comes to Right-Sizing, "re" refers to the celebration of a new space found within an old home. You want your house to better fit how you and your family live now, and hopefully for years ahead. The challenge is to discover your home's new potential, in a series of exercises that open your eyes to possibility. Evaluate what can be done with the space you already have, then take action depending on your needs.

The 15 "re" words here should start your creative juices flowing. Have fun with them—you'll be surprised that you will think of many more "re" words on your own. May they inspire you to Right-Size your home!

THE ART OF
"RE"

REARRANGE (rē´-ə-rānj´) Before you move furniture around physically, move it around on a floor plan to see how it looks

RECLAIM (rē-klām´) Transform your seldom-used guest room by adapting it, creating your new and much-needed home office

RECYCLE (rē-sī´kəl) Take an old idea, such as a breakfast nook, and make a space-saving eating area in or near the kitchen

REDESIGN (rē´dĭ-zīn´) Think about creating more counter space in your kitchen, with a "prep" work island, that could be mobile or fixed in place

REDISCOVER (rē-dĭ-skŭv´ər) Remember your main floor powder room or half bath may have the potential to be converted into a full bath

REDUCE (rĭ-dōōs´) This is the perfect opportunity to get rid of your accumulated clutter, so you can better discover the space you have

REFRESH (rĭ-frĕsh´) Adapt your children's bath or baths into a safe and sound room, with grab bars and skid-resistant flooring

REIMAGINE (rē-ĭ-măj´ĭn) Pick an unused room, such as the living room, and create another name for it, such as the chat room

REINVENT (rē´ĭn-vĕnt´) Turn the back door area—the real family entry—into a mudroom that better suits your family's needs

REMOVE (rĭ-mōōv´) Change your closet around so that clothing and shoes can be easily seen and reached; move out-of-season items into another closet or storage unit

RENEW (rĭ-nōō´) Convert your too-formal dining room; make it more relaxed with a large round or square table instead of a rectangle

REPLACE (rĭ-plās´) Substitute that bedroom armoire and huge TV for a flat screen version with a sleeker chest beneath, to hold the equipment

RETHINK (rē-thĭngk´) Turn a wide hallway into a study hall, where there is room for multiple computers, shared equipment, and parental supervision

RETRIEVE (rĭ-trēv´) Save your laundry from being only a workspace; make it multifunctional, including crafting or entertaining service area

REVIVE (rĭ-vīv´) Perk up your family room with a sectional to replace the aging sofa and chairs; this will allow everyone to have a relaxing space to sprawl

How To Use This Book

THINK OF *RIGHT-SIZING YOUR HOME* **AS YOUR FRIEND.** It was written with the idea that you will be able to rethink the rooms in your house, and make them fit your lifestyle. There is a lot of helpful advice to consider. This book assists you in making the ultimate decisions to change a room or two—or three—much easier.

Each chapter is centered on a function in the house, such as bathing, relaxing, or eating. For example, most eating does not take place in the formal dining room anymore. Think about the areas of the house where you *do* eat. These spaces need to be adapted to meet your actual eating style. It may be breakfast in your bedroom, or even bathroom, lunch in the kitchen, and supper in front of the TV. Perhaps that dining room needs to be recycled for a more frequently-used purpose.

If you spot some products you like, you'll find retailer's and manufacturer's information in the "Resources" chapter on page 200.

Right-Sizing Tools In Each Chapter

Style Audit A set of questions to ponder about your lifestyle, as it relates to the activity covered in the chapter. Certain actions or habits define specific personalities. You select the personalities, or combination of them, that best describes you and your family members.

Trade-Offs A comparison of possible design options and how they can affect your needs versus your wants.

Measuring Up An essential schematic reference that illustrates various spatial arrangements within rooms.

Redesign Plan A worksheet that leads you through an examination of the uses and requirements of your space.

Now It's Your Turn A selection of ideas to help you think, rethink, and think again about your Right-Sizing goals.

What You Need To Get Started

You need five simple things to begin the process of Right-Sizing your home.

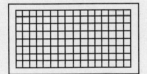

Tape Measure

Graph Paper

Brown Paper Bags

An Open Mind

Willingness To Change Your Home

a s you read the few pages that follow, you will see that the first three items are necessary tools in understanding your existing rooms, and in showing you the possibilities for change—*before* you start purchasing new furniture, cabinetry, or even accessories. While I cannot personally assure you that you won't slip-up, I know that if you use the tape measure, graph paper, and paper bags, you are less likely to have a major mistake on your hands.

Keep an open mind and forget the words of that real estate agent still ringing in your ears: *You must have a dedicated dining room and living room.* Change "must have" to "had" and you are halfway there. Rooms can always be converted to their original purpose if resale is an issue, but chances are good any potential buyer will like your vision of true livability.

Lastly, the willingness to change is a quality you must find within yourself. It's a tricky one because changes to a home, no matter how big or how small, always affect every member of the family. Of course, getting everyone to agree may not be easy, but when they actually see a reinvention of their room or rooms, change will be easier to support. Summon the courage to Right-Size and I'll wager everyone will love the results.

How To Measure

IT MAY SEEM BIZARRE TO DEVOTE SEVERAL pages to a subject you think you already know! However, one of the principles of Right-Sizing is to clearly understand the space you have, and this requires accurate measuring, sometimes remeasuring. This will also involve creating a floor plan, something you may not already know.

In order to make your rooms work better for you, you *must* rethink the space in these rooms. You'll need to look again at features you've probably ignored over time:

- *Do your rooms all feel squarish, or are they imperfectly shaped with niches or bump-outs, or both?*
- *Are there radiators, columns, or a fireplace that dominate the space?*
- *Are windows, doors, or other openings getting in the way of where you want to place the furniture?*
- *Does the room have a chair rail or other molding that protrudes into the room?*

The first step is the floor plan. Think of it as a portrait of your room or rooms as they are right now. It's a detailed picture from which you can plainly see your useable floor space, and the truth is it will help you be objective. It will be easier to visualize your new seating arrangement, the layout of your innovative workspace, or that kitchen you've been designing in your mind.

You don't have to be an artist, just start with a rough sketch of the room. Begin in one corner of the room and draw an outline of the floor. Add every window and door, as well as anything that is built-in, like a bookcase or fireplace, along with niches and bump-outs. Continue around until you have sketched the entire room. This becomes your worksheet.

Starting from the same corner where you began your sketch, carefully measure. You will need the overall dimensions of each wall—the width and length of the room. Be sure to write down each measurement as you go along. It's almost impossible to remember all the individual numbers, if you don't put them immediately in the appropriate place on your sketch.

The next step is to measure each wall again. This time you will measure the details of the room, from that first corner to the first protrusion—be it a window, door, radiator, alcove, or bookcase. Measure those too, as you continue around the room until you return to your initial corner.

To double-check your measurements, the length and width of the room should agree with the total individual measurements of each wall you just completed. If the measurements do not add up, then remeasure to see where you went wrong.

The last step is to determine the height of the room, and its details, and record them on your sketch as well. For example, measure from the floor to the bottom of each window, or the top of each door. Then measure from the bottom to the top of each window. Also, measure from the top of the door or window to the ceiling. Continue around the room until all openings are recorded. Make sure each set of measurements equal the overall height of the wall.

How To Make A Floor Plan

THAT WAS THE HARD PART— NOW IT GETS
much easier. You are going to translate all your careful
measurements onto quarter-inch graph paper.

Each square of the graph paper will represent one
foot. For example, if the room measures 10½ feet wide
and 12 feet long, mark out 12 vertical squares and 10½
horizontal squares. (You may want to work in a larger
scale, e.g. ½ inch = 1 foot.) If you color in each square
you used, this will clearly indicate your floor space.

Write the scale in one corner of the graph paper:
¼ inch = 1 foot. In an opposite corner, indicate the
overall measurements of the room.

Now include the door and windows as well as other
architectural features, including columns, fireplaces,
and radiators on the floor plan. Indicate what, and
where, these built-ins are located.

Double-check your measurements with what you
have drawn on the paper. Everything should add up;
if it doesn't, grab that tape measure again. You might
have written down a wrong measurement somewhere
along the way. Find the mistake, correct it. Measure
again just to make sure. Now you have a great tool in
your hand—an accurate plan of the room. Make four or
five copies, and always keep a copy in your handbag,
notebook, or briefcase. You never know when you just
might need it for reference.

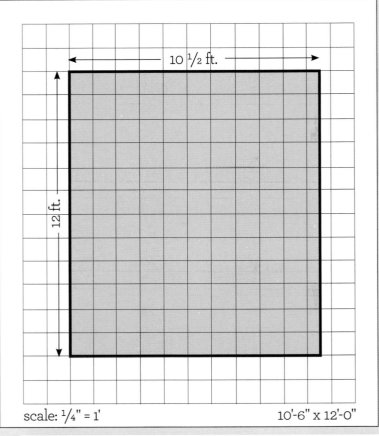

10 ½ ft.

12 ft.

scale: ¼" = 1'   10'-6" x 12'-0"

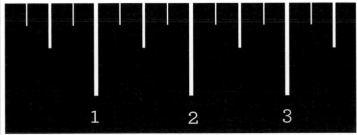

1   2   3

How To Create A Furniture Plan

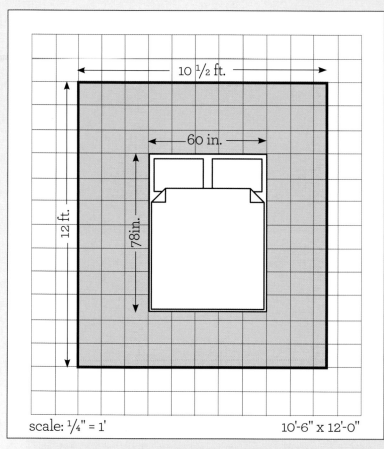

10 ½ ft.

60 in.

12 ft.

78 in.

scale: ¼" = 1'   10'-6" x 12'-0"

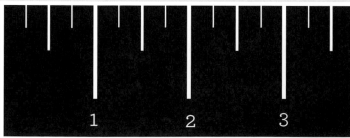

1   2   3

USING ANOTHER PIECE OF GRAPH PAPER, create cutouts of your existing furniture or cabinets, as well as your rugs. Measure each piece as you did your room, and create a model using the same scale that you did for the room. For example, your queen-size bed and frame may measure 60 inches (5 feet) by 78 inches (6½ feet). This means your drawing will be 5 horizontal squares by 6½ vertical squares. Be sure to label each drawing, indicate the room it's in, and make a few copies. You will use them for your plan for this room, or another room you are planning to Right-Size.

Continue to measure all your furniture, transfer to graph paper, cut out, and label. Arrange all the pieces on a copy of your floor plan and when you're satisfied it is a fair representation of the room you are Right-Sizing, stick it down with double-face tape. Congratulations, you have a floor plan of your existing layout!

Use the other copies of the plan to try new furniture arrangements with your existing furniture. Put key pieces in their proposed new places, then add the others as you wish. This will help you see how, and if, a new arrangement might work, without actually moving around heavy furniture and destroying your back, or the floor, in the process.

If you are *rethinking* how this room might work by adding new or different pieces of furniture, get the measurements, draw the new pieces on graph paper, and make cutouts. Using another copy of the floor plan, apply the cutouts of the new pieces, along with existing pieces you plan to use, to see if it works.

You will then be able to see side by side comparisons of your different approaches to the room's function. It may also help you rethink the comfort and ease with which you move about the space.

How To Construct A Furniture Model

MOST OF US HAVE A HARD TIME, EVEN WITH
a floor plan in hand, visualizing new furniture in our
existing rooms. Somehow when we are in a furniture
store, antique store, or even an auction house we forget
how big or small the space is we are trying to fill.
Or worse, how the new piece will look in that space.
Understanding how this furniture will fit into the
available floor space is vital. Equally important is how
you will get it into your home. So it's back to the tape
measure again!

Before you even think about placing that order, get the
width, length, and height measurements of the furniture,
and head home. These numbers can represent the
difference between success and an unpleasant return to
the store.

Now—for the paper bag trick! Using several, regular
paper grocery bags (newspaper works as well), cut them
to lay flat and tape them together. Use the measurements
that you brought home and make an outline of the piece
you propose to buy, adding bags as needed. Arrange the
pattern in the area of the room you intend to place the
furniture. Seeing the model in conjunction with the rest
of your furniture will help you feel confident—or not—
about the purchase. Ask yourself the following questions:

o *Does the size overwhelm the existing furniture?*
o *Will it be easy to move around it?*
o *Do you really have room for it?*
o *Can you open drawers or doors of the piece
without interference?*
o *Is the scale too small for the room?*
o *Is it in proportion to the rest of the room?*
o *Does it interfere with other furniture?*

Okay, that was part one. Once you are satisfied
the furniture will work in the room, on to part two—a
potential deal-breaker. This part requires help from
someone else. You are going to trace the trail through
your home that this new piece of furniture would travel to
get to its assigned room.

Holding the paper bag model flat, as you would a
piece of actual furniture, see how it fits coming through
your main entry, down a hall or up stairs, around a corner,
and even the doorway of the room where it will live. If
you live in an apartment, try this model in your elevator
as well. More fine pieces of furniture have sat in building
lobbies, because this measurement was not taken into
consideration. Better you discover the problems with
access before you make a purchase.

All may not be lost. Some sofas, for example, come
with removable or boltable arms. Larger pieces, such as
bookcases or even china cabinets, are often constructed
in parts. Be sure to ask the right questions of your
salesperson—not just what the piece measures, but
whether it needs to be disassembled and reassembled
(and how much that might cost). The whole point is to
make sure you have all the necessary details to ensure a
safe and happy delivery.

How to Right-Size

Step #1 – Evaluate Your Needs

Getting Your Act Together

I**T'S ALL TOO EASY TO COMPLAIN** that your house doesn't work for you, and that you should think about moving or maybe renovating. Both are daunting prospects, especially these days. Maybe just stay where you are and fume? Nonsense! You can—and should—do something about your living situation. Your home should be all you want it to be. Your home should have the room you need. For example, if you're not dining formally, then do you *need* a dining room or are you actually eating in the family room most of the time? Your home should fit your and your family's lifestyles.

There are remedies that don't require such drastic measures as complete renovation or actually moving. Start with one room. Take a step back and try to envision it as though you have never seen the room before; as though you were someone else, walking in for the first time. How would that person react if you weren't within earshot? Too scary, perhaps to be so objective, but necessary.

How about taking photos of the room? A couple of shots of the whole room, from different points of view, plus a couple of details will suffice. Don't move things around first, and don't put things away that are always visible. Take honest photos. When you finally look at them, it will be like seeing yourself in a three-way dressing room mirror, when no one else is looking. What do you see?

A worn out sofa covered with a blanket to hide the dog fur, or a stained carpet that's created its own new patterns? Some mismatched lamps that hardly illuminate the room, or a lumpy chair whose springs are about to burst through the seat? Have you been ignoring all this, or have you simply refused to undertake the task of making improvements? No matter, you're about to start—right now!

The first step in learning how to Right-Size is to evaluate how (and if) this room is actually used. Forget about the furniture disaster you just uncovered; this is more important. You are going to make a list for your eyes only, with the understanding there are no right answers—only the truth. **List all the ways you currently use this room, no matter what the room's name really is**.

For example, if you are focusing on the family room, what else do you do there besides watch TV? Do you read, do puzzles, listen to music, or play games? Maybe this is your workspace during the day when no one else is at home? Admit it, many evening meals are eaten in front of that large TV. How about the kids: do they do their homework there? Is this where friends and family gather when you're entertaining? It is, of course, a hangout for the dog or cat when no one is looking—put that down as well.

Okay, now let's make another inventory. **This second list is about how you *would like* to use this room**. Maybe you need one area of the room for homework, both yours and the children's. Another area might be dedicated to entertainment, in a more organized space, instead of spread all over as it might be now. You get the idea.

Instead of trying to cram all the family activities into this space, why not consider moving some of the quieter recreations to another room? Folding your laundry or doing some of your craft projects could easily be shifted elsewhere. Reading, especially if it competes with the TV, should probably move out of this space as well.

Now, compare the two lists (how the room is used and how you would like the room to work) and see if they agree or compete. Slowly but surely, you will develop a plan of action. As you study the plan, other rooms will come into play since you have started to consider moving certain activities to those areas. Keep the lists, notes, and photos in a folder—"Getting My Act Together in the Family Room."

Repeat the process with each of the other rooms in your home that need rethinking, keeping a folder for each. When you're finished, you will have created a comprehensive plan.

What you have just done is **evaluate your needs**. Turn the page and begin Step #2.

1

1 2 3 4 5

Step #2 – Envision The Arrangement

Determining What You *Really* Need

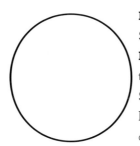

NCE YOU HAVE COMPLETED Step #1—**Evaluating Your Needs**—you are ready for the next step in the Right-Sizing process. This is a little more difficult, but not overwhelming. You might need the **assistance of a trusted friend** or family member, who can be the voice of your conscience in this process.

Take out the pad and pen again, and walk through that room one more time. Look at it with fresh eyes. Now start *mentally* weeding out items in the room. The good news is, at this point, you don't have to actually move anything. You are just assessing the contents and beginning to **imagine the space in its new incarnation**.

Now, two more lists. First, list everything you absolutely need to keep in this space. Then list what you think should be removed, either permanently or simply shifted to another area.

This will give you a sense of what needs to be replaced or added, whether a new purchase or relocated from another room. If you have created a floor plan (as you learned in the preceeding chapter), you can better envision the space, including how to deal with built-ins such as a fireplace or bookcases.

Here's where the good friend (GF) comes in. It's one thing to mentally weed out your possessions, and quite another to physically begin the process. Even if you don't particularly like that chair or rug, you may be emotionally attached to it. Do you remember where you bought it? Are there memories of that rug in your grandmother's house? The GF's job here is to remind you that the rug is moth-eaten, and has more than served its purpose. The GF has to be honest enough to motivate you. Nothing brutal, but they have to help you see the sofa has needed a new slipcover for ages, and that the rug has definitely got to go!

Now you can start the fun part—imagining how the room will look in its new life. Pull out that floor plan and little cutouts, and try the new furniture arrangement. Are there pieces in other parts of the house that would be perfect for this "new" room? Also, think about other spaces that would be improved if you could reuse some of what you have eliminated with this plan.

For example, let's say you've targeted the under-used and neglected dining room. Your need for a dedicated office is higher on your list of needs than eating in a formal setting once or twice a year. Start with the dining table, which is usually the largest piece of furniture in the house. Try to envision it as your desk (because it has great spread out space, which most home office desks are lacking). If it doesn't work for the layout you are creating, then mentally put it aside.

The chairs are not suitable for a home office. You need a mobile chair with proper support when working at your desk. Dining chairs can be moved to other locations and brought back if need be. The large china cabinet, buffet, or breakfront is a big question mark. Your GF suggests that you could retrofit the heirloom cabinet for storage of paper supplies and files.

Then GF reminds you that you probably do need the table twice a year (that's what friends are for!) and that it might make an appropriate desk if the leaves were removed and stored away. Now you also have a short list of things you need: a comfortable desk chair on casters, some discreet file cabinets, and a better computer—as opposed to buying a whole roomful of office furniture. With a little fiddling and disguising, the room can periodically return to functioning as a part-time dining room.

Congratulations! You have just really begun to Right-Size, and you have not moved a thing—except in your mind and on paper. You have completed Step #2 – **Envision the Arrangement**. Time to tackle Step #3.

1 **2** 3 4 5

Step #3 – The One-Two-Three Method

Getting Rid Of What You Don't Want

N O ONE HAS SAID THIS Right-Sizing business was going to be easy, but keep your goal in mind—a reinvented house that works better for you. By now, you should be buoyed by the enthusiasm of your vision, which—hopefully—you've shared with others in the family, and with friends. Their support and understanding cannot be underestimated and will help get you through this next step, the weeding-out process.

You are starting with one room today, and you will need to devote the better part of it to the sorting process. Count on your GF to help make the day a bit easier with some humor, and maybe some music to keep you energized. Looking forward to a glass of wine at the end of the day may serve as an incentive to keep moving. Of course, the real reward will be the reclaimed space—maybe lost years ago and never thought of since.

Begin in one corner and stay with that area until you complete sorting there. Slowly but surely, move to the next trouble spot. You are going to **create three piles** as you work through your possessions. Let's call this the **One-Two-Three Method**.

The first pile will be your "yes" pile, which means you are keeping everything in it. Tag it or use a sticky note to indicate where it is to go when you're finished. You might want to color code the room locations for easier transfer.

The next pile of belongings will be the "no" pile, and these belongings will either be donated, sold, stored elsewhere, or tossed. Depending on your willpower, this stack should be of equal size to the previous "yes" pile. You can come back to this mound later, to make decisions about where the items will head.

The third pile is the "maybe" mound, and this is where you should place items whose fate you can't decide at the moment. Watch that most of your things don't wind up here. GF needs to be on the ball here and keep this pile at a minimum, but to keep you going, he or she should move the undecided possessions in that "maybe" pile—*temporarily*.

The objective is to get through the contents of the room as quickly and efficiently as possible. Better to sort the big items first such as chairs or tables. The more you linger, the more sentimentality can start clouding your judgment. Don't be tempted.

There are stories to be told about much of what you have, but perhaps the stories are what you want to hold onto—not the actual thing. If that's the case, take a photo of the item and preserve it in an **album of precious possessions** from which those stories can be retold. The good part is that you don't have to clean or dust what's in the album, and they don't take up valuable real estate. Maybe you can pass these pieces along to the next generation, or a family member who would be the new caretaker.

Whether you're dealing with a closet, cabinet contents, or just general clutter, you're going to feel much better by the end of the day. Strangely enough, despite the emotional roller coaster of reexamining your things, there is a sense of lightening your load. The clearing-out frees you from the tyranny of too much stuff.

It's best to stay with this sort, dump, or store method. You can't possibly tackle everything in a day, but at the end of that day there should be little or nothing in the "maybe" pile, and more in the "no" than in the "yes" pile. The feeling of progress should spur you on to continue with the **One-Two-Three Method**. Remember the goal of the sorting process: to get rid of what you *really* don't need.

Good going! Now you can move onto Step #4.

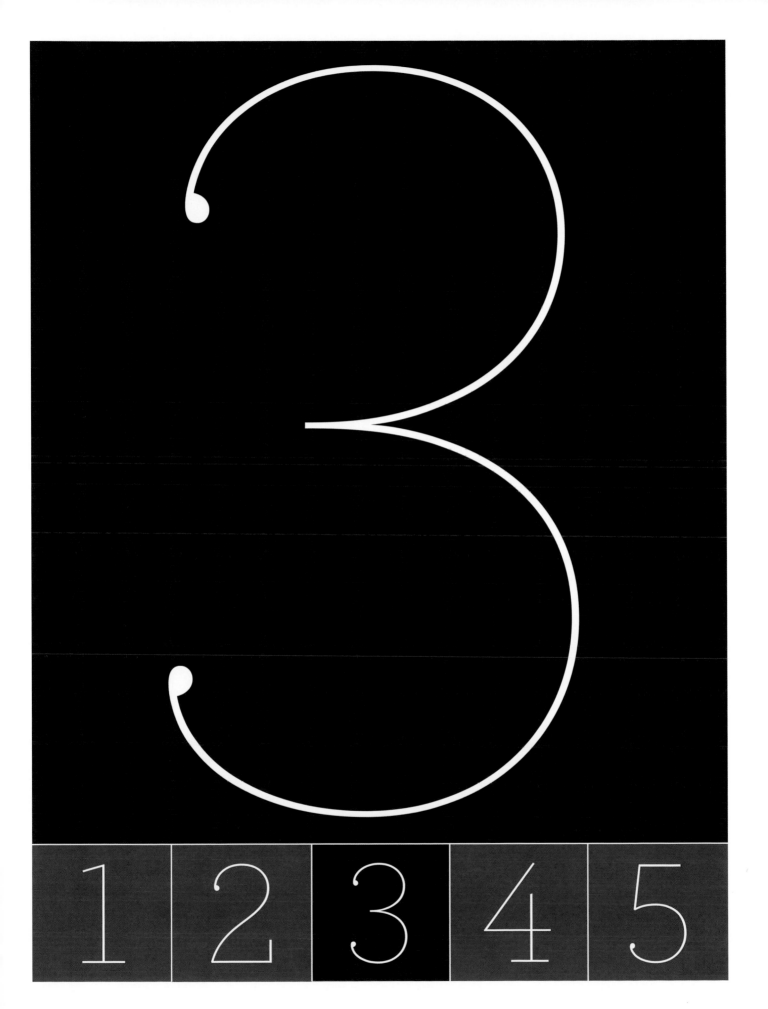

Step #4 – The Just-Right Space
Using The Space Wisely And Well

ERHAPS YOU SKIMMED through the previous steps, but this is one step you absolutely cannot ignore. Okay, maybe you did work through steps one, two, and three but perhaps not as precisely as you had hoped. In fact, there still might be unresolved items in the "maybe" pile. Time to decide and move on, or you will be forever stuck in the sorting process.

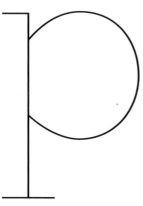

By now you have removed, recycled, or replaced the old furniture that's not a part of your plan for this space. Donating these pieces to a good cause is a great idea, but don't forget to check with your children, other family members, or even friends who might want to repurpose your treasures. Certainly you could move some of the pieces to another room in your home, but only if you have a valid place for the relocation! Don't just clear out one room only to clutter up another. That defeats the purpose of your efforts.

Make sure the unnecessary accessories and lamps follow suit. There is nothing worse than having a noticeable flaw in your new room. For example, if it's your dining room you are Right-Sizing into a home office, I'll bet the crystal chandelier no longer seems quite right. Wouldn't it look great in your entrance hall? Or perhaps you might want to add a bit of glamour to your bathroom.

If recycling is not possible, the alternative is to dispose of the orphan pieces as quickly as possible. Otherwise they might turn up elsewhere. The worst case scenario is they end up back in the orginal room!

As long as you're working on a fresh purpose for the space, you might consider adding at least one new design aspect. Painting the walls, replacing the window treatments, or even trading in the carpet for a great rug, can be an instant signal to anyone who uses or visits this room, that it is indeed a "new" place. The change doesn't have to break the bank, but it should be special enough to make you want to celebrate your eventual Right-Sizing achievement.

Now that some things have been cleared out, **work with your floor plan** and bring in the new pieces one by one. Place the largest or bulkiest in the space you envisioned. Does it work? Is it too crowded, too close to other pieces? Is there room to easily pass by? The answers to these questions should be yes, no, and yes, in that order.

If you used the paper bag model ("How to Construct a Furniture Model," page 23), you already knew it would work, the room would not be too crowded, and traffic would comfortably flow.

But if you're having an "Oops!" moment, it probably means you didn't follow that paper bag advice before you moved the piece of furniture that now won't fit into the alcove! Take a breath and promise yourself to always make a furniture model first. There's no sense moving heavy or bulky things if you don't have to.

Now it's time to bring in the rest of what will complete Right-Sizing the room into a fresh new space. There will be *that* moment, when you step back and feel a sense of pride. You did it! Your room has been Right-Sized. It's just as you imagined it, and now it makes sense for others who use it as well. You have created **The Just-Right Space,** and completed Step #4 .

Hopefully your success in this room will motivate you to continue Right-Sizing through other spaces. You can make your entire home work better for you. Think of this process as a game of dominoes—one completed room automatically leads to another.

But wait! There's just one more step. Before you sit back and relax, take a quick look at Step #5.

Step #5 – The Fifteen-Minute Rule

Maintaining The Right-Sizing

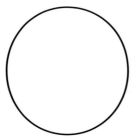

NCE YOU'VE SUCCEEDED in transforming your rooms into Right-Sized spaces that really work for you and your family, you'll no doubt want to sit back and just enjoy it. You worked hard to make this the place you wanted to be, so go ahead, take some pleasure in your accomplishment!

While you're admiring your handiwork, put this little mantra in your brain: *Maintain, maintain, or it will never look this way again.* The truth is that you, and others in your family, will begin leaving things around. At first just a few papers, a couple of unopened bills, or some newspapers find their way in. Then the catalogs reappear, but who really has the time to look through them? How about the pile of magazines that sit there neglected and unread? You simply can't throw them out without a glance or two...or three. Coupons seem to multiply without ceasing, and that pile of must-read books has continued to proliferate. Whatever it is, you have to be vigilant, so this Right-Sized room doesn't return to Clutter Central. All your good work will simply disappear.

Kitchens, family rooms, and home offices are, not surprisingly, giant magnets for the stuff of our lives. Despite all good intentions, everyone leaves it where it lands until, finally, chaos rules. Sound familiar? Or are you successfully keeping up with the threats to your well organized, Right-Sized space by refiling papers, recycling newspapers and magazines, and reducing the unnecessary stuff before it all becomes a permanent fixture?

Do you need a little help in this area? Reread the "Art of Re" (page 6). Remember that "re" words can get you back on track, and help you **keep the new space cleared and cleaned**. Repeat that phrase again:

Maintain, maintain, or it will never look this way again!

Here's the secret of how to manage the onslaught of clutter. You need only fifteen minutes, but this is a weekly commitment. Take those fifteen, undisturbed minutes and **work your way around the room**. Pick up the newspapers, catalogs, and magazines, and put them in the recycling bin. If they've been there for seven days, chances are you're not going to read them. If there are articles you simply must keep, clip them out and discard the remains.

Gather up all the loose papers and put them in a stack in one central "mound" on a chair—to be sorted as soon as possible. Unopened bills (who doesn't have a few of those?) and unread mail go in another, smaller heap. This might take priority over the previous stack. Be courageous: open everything. At least you'll get rid of the envelopes. Sort them into "handle today" and "handle later" piles.

Countertops or work surfaces seem to be additional areas where stuff accumulates. Don't just sweep it aside. Sort, store, and dispose of most of it, if not all. Find new homes for castoffs. Throw away out-of-date clippings, or notes to yourself that no longer make sense. Do you really need a list of great movies to see from 1999? Get rid of it along with the sales fliers that pile up your mail box.

The clock should still be ticking, unless you're engrossed in the mail or a magazine article. What else is in the room making it seem less organized? How about that abandoned pair of shoes? Maybe an empty coffee mug or two? Whatever it is, get it out of the room. Fifteen minutes are up!

Fifteen minutes times fifty-two weeks, means that in only about thirteen hours a year you can keep that Right-Sized room in far better shape than if you ignore it. That makes the **Fifteen-Minute Rule** really doable. You just have to decide to do it! Now you have time to focus on Right-Sizing another room in your home.

1 2 3 4 5

Public Spaces

Redefining our homes has put us in a quandry. What are we to do with formerly busy spaces, such as living and dining rooms? The kitchen is now the hub of the house. Eating has replaced dining, and we do it throughout the home. The same goes for relaxing. Depending on how you define the term, you can be happy in the basement or the bedroom, as well as the family room. Right-Sizing will help you get better control of the overused as well as the underused.

Where You Cook

The kitchen has always been "hospitality central." *It really doesn't matter how big your kitchen is, whether it's pint-sized or giant, economy-sized. This is the warm, welcoming place where all your friends and everyone in your family, especially those four-legged members, want to be.*

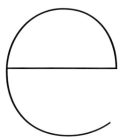

VEN BACK IN THE CAVEMAN DAYS, THE place where you cooked was where you lived. Now, with all the up-to-the-minute conveniences—and then some—the heart of the home is still the kitchen. There was, of course, a moment in time when cooking was something relegated to a closed kitchen, while guests waited in the living room for dinner to be served. It would have never occurred to your mother or grandmother to show off her workplace. Heavens, no! Gone are those days; now your guests can watch you as you work.

We have come a long way from that kind of thinking; now everyone uses the kitchen as "their" space. From the hurried breakfast, to relaxing with a cup of coffee, through after-school snacking, to a late-night foray to the refrigerator, the multitasking kitchen hardly has an idle moment.

Many kitchens expanded in the late 1980s into enormous party places, as the walls around them came tumbling down. The party is somewhat over now, and we need to take a good look at our culinary needs and what really works for us.

Cooking, reheating, brewing, or some variation happens in other locations as well. There are mini-kitchens or snack centers near the media room, or in a guest suite or a bonus room over the garage. For some, the full kitchen is nearly duplicated on a patio or deck during the warmer months. Let's not forget that wondrous concept—the morning kitchen tucked right next to the master suite. No caveman ever dreamed of this!

Not all of us have kitchens the size of a ballroom, or an open-plan home that permits a giant-sized culinary center. It takes just as much planning to turn a cozy, compact kitchen into a hard-working space, as it does an ample one. Wherever it is that you cook, reheat, grill, or have a cup of tea, may it serve you well, be functional, and always work in your favor.

And don't forget a canister of doggie biscuits!

> **HOME COOKING**
>
> *Today's kitchen is a gathering place. Convenient, built-in seating in the center makes a comfortable perch for watching the cook, eating, doing homework, or just relaxing.*

Cooking Style Audit

Select the style that best reflects your approach to cooking. Then follow the tips below for creating more space and order, suited to that style.

ARE YOU A SPECIALIZED COOK?

- O Use the kitchen as a hobby place for your cooking forté
- O Need a place for everything
- O Must have appliances geared for best results

TIPS:

- Lower part of the work surface to 27 inches if you are kneading or rolling out dough, or doing a lot of handwork, to relieve back strain
- Locate small appliances in one central place for efficient use, but don't leave them out on the counter if not used daily

- Consider the best appliances for your needs: ones with better browning capabilities, precise-control burners, or extra freezer space
- Configure drawer space for small and large supplies; plan for enough drawers for utensils, and deeper drawers to hold specialty bakeware or cookware

ARE YOU A GREAT ENTERTAINER?

- O Love to cook for family and friends
- O Kitchen is like a theater
- O Need an open kitchen to show off appliances

TIPS:

- Allocate enough counter space for cooking, serving, and cleanup; keep 24 to 36 inches between appliances
- Allow enough cabinet room for frequently-used china and serving pieces; store occasional-use items in an easy-access pantry, or close by—but not in the kitchen

- Plan on a second sink for preparation and cleanup; add a disposal to this unit to simplify waste removal
- Make sure guests are comfortably seated in the kitchen, but not in your way where you prepare food.

ARE YOU A CO-CHEF?

- O Adapt to two different cooking styles
- O Utensils and appliances do not compete for space
- O Avoid bottleneck of activity at sink, stove, or counter

TIPS:

- Plan sufficient work surface for kitchen sharing; allow 24 to 36 inches per person for "spread space"
- Consider separate work areas, if space allows, keeping individual cooking supplies at hand; don't let them clog the kitchen

- Divide sink time, or allow 18 to 25 inches for a small second sink; alternatively, install a triple bowl sink (allowing at least 36 inches)
- Determine each person's cookware needs, then store efficiently in one, easily accessible cabinet

ARE YOU AN EVERYDAY FEEDER?

- O No time for fussing in the kitchen
- O Usually make tried-and-true recipes
- O Need everything at hand, without rummaging around

TIPS:

- Have all cooking supplies at your fingertips by planning enough cabinet space to store basic ingredients, or create an in-cabinet pantry area if you lack space for a separate one
- Make the most of space around the cooktop, oven, and microwave so pots and pans are readily available

- Upgrade your auxiliary appliances (large toaster oven or crock-pot), and make room for them on the counter if used frequently
- Don't forget a slip-resistant floor, which is important when you are in a hurry

ARE YOU A FAST FOODIE?

- O Need the minimum amount of pots and pans
- O Make use of microwavable dishes and leftover storage
- O Kitchen is a place to reheat

TIPS:

- Put microwave supplies near microwave or oven, making reheating effortless; allow about 6 by 12 by 5 inches for each container
- Store leftover food in containers in the refrigerator or freezer; be sure they are clearly marked with date of purchase

- Create adequate space for recycling cans, bottles, cardboard, and Styrofoam containers
- Keep additional, emergency foodstuffs on hand for quick meals; stock no-cook fruits and vegetables as supplementary menu items

Great Entertainer
Chef's Choice

F THE COOKING PROCESS IS PART OF
the entertainment in your home, remember an open-plan, party kitchen requires space—and lots of it. An island configuration, featuring the cooktop, range, or sink, allows you to face your audience. Any performer will tell you to never turn your back on them, even if they're friends.

The secret to an entertaining kitchen is comfortable, soft, barstool seating on the non-working side of the island. This keeps your guests at a safe distance, but more importantly, keeps them from getting under foot, unintentionally or otherwise.

Barstools no longer have a negative connotation—not since the kitchen has become "hospitality central." They provide perfect seating, bridging the gap between the viewing and working areas of your kitchen. Stools are generally available in two heights: 30 inches for a bar-height counter of 40 to 42 inches, and 24 to 25 inches for a 36-inch counter height. Remember to allow 10 to 12 inches between the stool seat, and the counter or table. This is important whether you are actually sitting with a drink, or just perching to chat.

Without a doubt, a party kitchen needs high-end appliances to inspire your inner chef. These are certainly part of the "show," and should offer impressive results. An oversized professional cooktop or range might be your first choice, but don't forget to leave room for an ample refrigerator (or two smaller ones) for

CENTER STAGE

Provide cushy seating around an island for your hungry guests and they will appreciate your cooking even more. They need to be in very easy reach of the hors d'oeuvres!

CHEF'S SPECIAL

A versatile pantry disguised as a British-style larder, keeps many supplies close at hand.

FEELING SAUCY

Organize cookware in a pullout base drawer. Pegs hold everything in place.

CLEAN MACHINE

If you have enough room, install a smaller, second dishwasher to handle extra cleanup.

ingredients, drinks, and snacks. Some kitchen islands are designed with refrigerated drawers, keeping prepared ingredients at hand. If space permits, twin dishwashers are ideal for stashing dirty dishes, as you move through each aspect of the menu.

The third most essential element in a party kitchen is *quiet* appliances. This means you will need a great exhaust system, with a vent that is powerful enough to remove both cooking odors and steam, without being too noisy. There is nothing worse than having to talk above the sound of a noisy fan. This is true of some dishwashers as well, which can be quite intrusive if you must run it while guests are still in attendance. The normal conversation level is 58 to 60 decibels, so look for dishwashers and stove hoods that operate below 56 decibels.

Let's not forget a commodious sink that gives you adequate space for preparation, as well as cleanup. Faucets have reached new heights in design. With architectural spouts and restaurant-style flexibility, they are easy to grasp and thorough in their task.

Next, there are all the latest and greatest extras to ponder: built-in coffee machines, steam ovens, teppanyaki griddles, and three-zone wine refrigerators. The possibilities are mind-boggling, and expensive.

If your kitchen space isn't much larger than a breadbox, don't despair. There is hope for your entertainment endeavors! You can still include some features of the entertainer's kitchen. Focus on ample counter space to satisfy the entertainer in you. The good news is that many luxury manufacturers have scaled some of their appliances to fit more modest spaces. For example, both a high-end, drawer-style dishwasher and refrigerator can work in a smaller kitchen configuration.

While the wine refrigerator or built-in coffee maker may not work without sacrificing something else, in a smaller kitchen, these kinds of supplementary appliances might be located in a pantry or, believe it or not, in a nearby laundry room.

While you certainly need room to entertain in grand style, your kitchen is only as good as the skills of the chef. No matter the size, let your guests sit back and enjoy the show! ●

Kitchen Redesign Plan

Before you start planning to change your kitchen, look at the lists below. The items you check should help guide you in assessing your space, and how it might work best for you. Use these responses to define the problems, as well as the solutions.

Reasons for making a change?

(check all that apply)

○ Kitchen is too small
○ Arrangement is not functional
○ Lack of storage and/or counter space
○ Appliances are outdated or energy inefficient
○ Traffic pattern problems
○ Countertop is worn or dated
○ Insufficient hot water supply
○ Inadequate lighting or electrical outlets
○ Cabinets or hardware need repair

Who uses this room?

(check all that apply)

○ Adults
○ Older adults
○ Children
○ Guests
○ Pets

How is it used?

(check all that apply)

○ Meal preparation and cleanup
○ Eating family meals
○ Entertaining only
○ Both everyday and guest meals
○ Laundry
○ Homework
○ Paying bills/computer center
○ Phone and message center
○ Recycling center

What do you need to store here?

(check all that apply)

○ Everyday foodstuffs
○ Gourmet or specialty items
○ Pots, pans, and utensils
○ China and glassware
○ Serving platters and trays
○ Cleaning supplies
○ Paper supplies
○ Recycling items
○ Pet supplies

○ Bulk items

What do you need for more comfort?

(check all that apply)

○ More counter space
○ More storage space
○ Work island
○ Energy efficient appliances
○ Larger appliances
○ Duplicate appliances
○ Second sink
○ Separate pantry
○ Better lighting
○ Good ventilation
○ Separate workspaces, if shared
○ Adequate eating space
○ Slip-resistant flooring
○ Nearby door to outside
○ Child-proof cabinets
○ Room for casual guest or family seating
○ Accessible cabinets
○ Better traffic flow

Trade-Offs

As you map out a plan for Right-Sizing your kitchen, think about the trade-offs below. Remember to take into consideration the amount of space you really have, while weighing wants versus needs.

VERSUS

Island Work Center ←→ Kitchen Table
More storage space / Loss of storage space

Double Bowl Sink ←→ Second Sink
Takes less space / Takes up more work surface

Stove or Range ←→ Cooktop and Oven
Space saver / More convenient for two cooks

One Dishwasher ←→ Two Dishwashers
Space saver / Great for parties/holidays

Standard Dishwasher ←→ Dishwasher Drawers
Space maker / More efficient washing

VERSUS

Refrigerator/Freezer ←→ Separate Appliances
Space saver / Allows for more food storage

Bottom-Mount Fridge ←→ Top-Mount Fridge
Easier access to fresh food / Less bending for frozen food

In-Door Ice Dispenser ←→ Interior Ice Maker
Quicker access to ice / Less expensive to operate

In-Cabinet Pantry ←→ Freestanding Pantry
Easier access to supplies / Larger storage space

3

ON DISPLAY

Glass-front cabinets make a kitchen feel larger. They also show off more than you may want to display. Consider ribbed or etched glass instead, modifying the view.

Everyday Feeder

Home Cooking

OW LONG DOES IT really take to prepare a meal? When you factor in the time it takes to shop for all the ingredients, and the actual food preparation, it's a scary thought. Time is not your friend when it comes to fixing supper.

Your busy schedule includes your own workday, plus the before and after: dropping the children off at school,

running errands, picking up the children, delivering and picking them up for various activities...it goes on! Then home to fix nutritious meals that everyone will enjoy. Admittedly there are shortcuts to putting a meal on the table, and you're willing to take them when necessary— maybe every night?

If this is a close description of your life, you are an Everyday Feeder. Your kitchen needs to be as hard-working as you are. Efficiency and durability are high on the list of requirements. Who has time for high-

maintenance surfaces, appliances that don't do their share of the work, or out-of-reach storage?

Is your kitchen like Grand Central Station? Probably. Take stock of the complete kitchen layout. Is your workspace confined to a specific area, so you can quickly focus on the cooking tasks at hand? Do you share the space with your kids and their friends, who are endlessly running in and out? Maybe the dog or cat likes to be with you, underfoot of course. If space permits, one way of creating a barrier between you and the traffic, is a peninsula or island. Even a portable unit on casters will help. This keeps everyone to one side while you assemble the evening meal.

Also, why is it that everyone swarms the refrigerator, even though the contents are pretty much what they were yesterday? Keep a mini-fridge away from your work center, and stocked with healthy snacks and beverages. It's a great way to avoid these traffic jams.

A large sink with an easy-to-use faucet can be one of your best friends when you're rushing around the kitchen. It's both the prep and cleanup center all in one, and if you have room for a double or triple bowl version, you can multitask to your heart's delight.

Even the finish on your cabinets should work for your harried life. A low-maintenance finish that can be instantly wiped clean of fingerprints or food smudges, is essential. Cabinet hardware should be selected with the same ease-of-care in mind. Avoid handles or pulls with tricky patterns and details, where jam, peanut butter, or ketchup can hide when you're not looking.

Most importantly, focus on your countertop material and color. This feature alone represents almost 30 percent of the color of your kitchen and sets the tone for the room. Today, maintenance must be effortless. Take the time to check upkeep requirements of granite, laminates, solid surfaces, and other options before you make your countertop choice. Easy maintenance is every bit as important as color.

There's no doubt you'll need very well organized storage to help you perform your nightly meal magic. Having food supplies, as well as cooking equipment, close at hand will save important steps when you are in a hurry. Workable storage can be built into the kitchen design or hidden in a freestanding closet.

No Everyday Feeder can work without a handy recycling center for those cans, bottles, and packaging materials. Get them out of sight and make that family meal happen. Time's up! ●

STORE AND ORDER

Even the smallest pantry can take pressure off the cook. Keep needed equipment nearby and off the countertop, when not in use.

WATER FEATURE

A pullout faucet makes preparation and cleanup, a lot easier.

Co-Chef
Group Effort

FANTASY ISLAND

A large island nicely accommodates more than one cook. It also makes a serving space for the results of your combined labor.

THAT SINKING FEELING

A multilevel, double bowl sink is a creative answer to sharing, rather than arguing over, the space.

PERHAPS IT STARTED while making Sunday breakfast. Everyone, or someone, wanted to get into the act. Then it became a tradition of sorts. Maybe you had some resident helpers who wanted to make cookies or brownies with you. However it started, once others got a sense of success in the kitchen, you ended up sharing the space.

Ideally, you are the main chef without a team of eager little cooks-in-the-making to complicate your creative process. Sporadically—or on a regular basis—you could be surrounded by a "support staff." Suddenly you're the Co-Chef! The other cook (or cooks) won't be helping you, but will be doing his or her own culinary thing, so you had better make changes in the kitchen to accommodate them.

Whether your kitchen is small or large, adding more cooks requires more space. This includes workspace, cooking space, and cleanup space, as well as pass-by space. Having an island workspace makes multi-person cooking much easier, but most often an island is not just a workplace. It may house a cooktop or stove, or sink and dishwasher. If that's the case, try to find another length of space that would allow people to work side by side.

Another bottleneck is at the sink. Why does everyone

seem to want in at the same time? Surely sticky hands don't occur simultaneously. The obvious answer is to install a second sink, to take the pressure off the main one. This also makes a good place for prep work. If this solution doesn't fit into your kitchen, consider a double or triple bowl sink instead of your existing single one. The latest, luxury design, multilevel sinks in stainless steel, composite, or enamel over metal, offer endless possibilities.

Having a second cooking space may sound like an extravagant idea, but it may improve the multiple chef cooking process, and calm flaring tempers because of too much crowding together. If your space allows for a small, two burner cooktop, you may be able to accommodate that Sunday breakfast chef with a space all their own. An alternate idea is to use small appliances resourcefully, to create a secondary cooking area. Use a waffle iron on its smooth side as a grill, or an electric frying pan as a fifth burner. Make sure you have space to store this equipment out of sight when not in use.

One of the challenges of a multi-cook kitchen, is making more efficient use of cabinet space. Since everyone will have access to the space, there should be agreement that equipment is put back where it belongs, after use.

Invest in cabinet accessories that allow better use of interior space. For example, many pots and pans that fit into the same space makes good storage sense. Pay attention to that lost corner storage cabinet as well. Are you getting on your hands and knees to root out the right pan? If so, create easy access to what lies inside. There are cabinet accessory companies that can outfit existing or new cabinets, to streamline storage.

One last thought: the more people interacting in the kitchen, the more likely an accident will happen. Watch for spills on counters or floors, or knife mishaps, especially if little ones are concerned. You may have to change your role from Co-Chef to supervisor, all for safety's sake and family harmony. ●

THE POINT OF IT

Knives can be a safety hazard at the best of times, but when two or more are cooking— watch out! Storing knives behind glass panels on the backsplash makes them easier to access without peril.

GOING TO POTS

A two-tiered pot rack that easily pulls out, makes co-cooking easier. Having the lids where they should be reduces likely squabbles.

Kid Smarts

REMEMBER MUD PIES?

Backyard delicacies come in all shapes and sizes—your very first effort at "making" food? You've come a long way from pretending, and now it's time to teach your own children for real. Taking the time to teach some basics is not only a great way for children to understand healthy eating, but it also creates very special family time.

What a feeling of success a small child has baking that first cake or batch of cookies, or making hamburger patties! To be a part of the cook's team, to help make part of the meal—no matter if it's a little overcooked or a bit overbrowned—the results are priceless!

Cooking with your children

LITTLE HELPER

Everyone likes to measure and prepare foods. That means you can taste test! Keep the messy ingredients in a smaller area, to avoid spreading them around.

PLAYTIME

To keep kids' activities close at hand but not underfoot, give them a lower cabinet area for their favorite toys and games.

does require careful supervision, time, and lots of patience. You'll need to overlook spilled milk or a flour-spattered floor, but isn't it better than mud pies in the backyard? Think of the math to be learned in measuring ingredients. How about the self-esteem gained in presenting the end product?

To most of us, the kitchen represents a wonderful place full of good and tasty things. Kids don't have to cook in the kitchen, but they like to be with you while *you* do, so give them a place to play. Create a toy corner, out of the way of traffic, or stock a low cabinet with plastic measuring cups and bowls for their own "cooking" project. This encourages their imagination in a safe, easily monitored area that will not interfere with your own job of getting a meal on the table.

Consider slip-resistant flooring and durable countertops, to combat the wear and tear kids inflict so innocently on the kitchen. Lower cabinets that contain breakable or dangerous supplies should be locked, so they are not easily accessible. Safety in the kitchen is another valuable lesson! ●

Specialized Cook
Test Kitchen

CAN YOU ADMIT that fixing a meal is only secondary to your real purpose in the kitchen? The trouble is that your hobby has become a passion, and now your kitchen must reflect this not-so-secret activity. Relax. Everyone has enjoyed tasting the fruits of your labors!

Whether your speciality is baking extraordinary cookies, whipping up a celebration cake, or creating a new generation of amazing jams, your kitchen was probably not designed to accommodate all the extra equipment your forté demands. Are you jammed-up with cake pans of all sizes and shapes, oversized cookie sheets, or an array of jelly jars? It

is now time to take control of your kitchen, before it gets worse.

Start with an inventory of what you need for everyday cooking. Can you reduce the number of old pots and pans, for the good cause of making room for your new bakeware? It may be a struggle, but once you grasp the contents of your cupboards, you can then rearrange them for better organization. Now extend your inventory to the foodstuffs and supplies you store. Would any of these items be better off in a nearby pantry—or more efficiently—in one cabinet, as opposed to being spread out over two or three?

Next, look at your workspace. Does it still work for you? Quite possibly, you have a crowd of small appliances dominating your countertops. Sort

NOW WE'RE COOKIN'

If space is tight, think about a smaller version of a pro's range.

PERSONAL STYLE

When your cooking method requires special storage, try semi-custom cabinets that can be modified to suit your needs. They can be adapted, without much difficulty, to fit the space.

them out, discarding what you don't frequently use. Can you also move those space-hogging canisters, which were just for show anyway, to a less important location? These are simple ways of creating needed space you forgot you had.

The countertop should reflect the activities of the Specialized Cook. Maybe you need a small marble insert, or a marble section of the countertop for rolling out pie dough, or a wooden board for kneading bread? If you are making a change of surface, chose one that works best for *all* your cooking needs.

A larger investment is in new appliances that make your life easier, and betters the results of your labors. Does the existing oven brown evenly? How about having a second oven? Do you have enough burner space on your cooktop? Is your refrigerator capable of handling all the chilling or storing you now require? How about a secondary freezer to handle extra supplies? Take a careful look at what's on the appliance market. You may not need (or even have room) for professional-sized appliances. The good news is that many of the luxury brands are now scaling down the dimensions of their machines. For example, you may find superior performance in a regular-sized stove

The old adage *a place for everything, and everything in its place*, is never more important than here and now. Getting yourself organized is time-consuming in the beginning, but will save you effort and running around

HIDDEN POTENTIAL

One of the latest trends in kitchen design is making heavier items more accessible. Your back will appreciate that those frequently used pots now move with ease.

in the long run. Group utensils that you use together. The same is true of baking pans, pots, or even decorating equipment. It sounds so basic, but most of us have a bad habit of scattering our tools in various drawers or containers.

The last step is putting it all together. That is, creating a special storage space for your culinary hobby. It makes sense to have everything together in one area, for easy access. Creating a baking center with your supplies and equipment may take some readjustment, but it will certainly work for you. Now let's get busy! ●

WELL-STOCKED

Some pantries are just too good-looking to hide away behind closed doors. Consider the objective of a storage closet is making sure everything can be clearly seen, and simply reached.

Measuring Up
Kitchen Dimension Guide

How much space do you really need to Right-Size your kitchen? Each drawing below shows a typical layout with minimum (MIN) and recommended (REC) values for comfort and usability. This information is for planning purposes only—be sure to check local or state building codes.

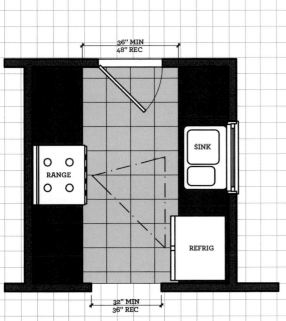

CORRIDOR KITCHEN

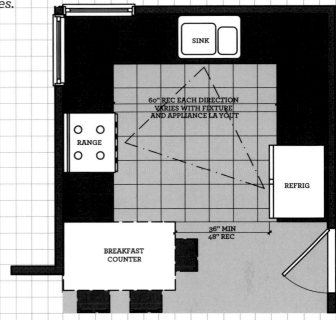

G-SHAPED KITCHEN

GENERAL TIPS:

- Refrigerator doors need to fully open to remove shelves, so allow extra space
- Keep sink, dishwasher, and trash bin close together for efficient cleanup

- A stand-alone cooktop creates a continuous countertop, with pot storage below
- In small kitchens, think small appliances; e.g., 18" wide dishwashers, 24" wide ranges, etc.
- Install tall wall cabinets for extra storage in a small kitchen

- Plan a counter close to the oven or refrigerator, for hot dishes and groceries
- Be sure to locate electrical outlets where needed
- Shorten or eliminate cabinets above sinks for greater comfort

---

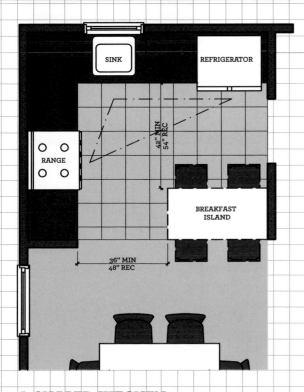

L-SHAPED KITCHEN

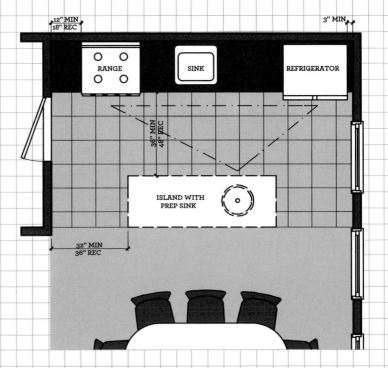

GALLEY KITCHEN

3

Fast Foodie

What's Cooking?

ET'S GET THE OBVIOUS over right now! Just say it: you do not like to cook. There must be a hundred reasons such as, "no time to shop, let alone cook," or " Mother never taught me." The truth is, when dinnertime rolls around, you would rather carry-in or call-in your meals. Thank goodness you have a great supermarket nearby, as well as the "usual suspects" of eating establishments in the neighborhood, offering take-out food. Put it on a pretty plate, and who's the wiser?

The real giveaway of the Fast Foodie is the number of cardboard or plastic containers of leftovers sitting in your refrigerator. At least you could get rid of the evidence! All kidding aside, there is a different set of kitchen requirements for you.

A smaller, well-organized kitchen is what you need, but what you want may be another story. Remember— you can walk up to 100 miles over a year's time in a larger-scaled kitchen, but the Fast Foodie is all about efficiency. The object is to get food on the table quickly. Think small, unless you have a partner, spouse, or child who regularly takes over the cooking duties.

Starting with appliances, your best buddy is the microwave, or new speed oven, which reheats so fast no one will have any idea you brought

BASKET CASE

Nothing can be faster than having food such as fruits, ready to eat. Keep them in your pantry, stored in pullout wicker baskets, as pick-up-and-go food.

COOKING LIGHT

A large counter makes this kitchen a pleasant place to assemble food into a delicious meal. A trash bin, stowed beneath the large sink, helps dispose of the evidence.

in dinner. Place it in a convenient location near your serving area, wherever that may be—in the island, at waist height, built into a wall of cabinets, or even over the stove. Cosmetics aside, all microwaves have the same function. Avoid a countertop model—it takes up too much space and competes with your smoothie blender.

You may covet a large stove or cooktop for its glamorous looks and sparkle, but do you really need it? Think smart, and save that extra space for a new bottom-mount refrigerator: a fridge with a maximum cooling or chilling area on the top, and a smaller freezer on the bottom to handle that frozen yogurt or some ice cubes. Be honest—you don't really need a great big refrigerator either. What you put in there usually stays there, hidden in the back, waiting to be discovered—and tossed out. Don't live with a larger repository for leftovers.

Ideally, what you *do* need, is a small pantry stocked with those serve-in-minutes packages ready to perform dinner miracles. Don't make it too big or too deep, or supplies may get lost in the back of the cabinet or closet. Put an assortment of microwave-safe containers and lids on your shopping list, and keep them handy. Do your heating in these containers, and get rid of the evidence of your secret source.

Last, but certainly not least, are some really good-looking plates or platters on which to arrange your food. This is where you can shine. Think of the tricks of a food stylist; use those handsome cloth napkins and the good flatware. And don't forget a simple garnish before serving. Who was it that said parsley is a girl's best friend? ●

SHELF AWARE

Don't clutter up your kitchen with foodstuffs you will never use. Install a slim, pullout pantry near the microwave, with enough power to handle an emergency meal.

THE HEAT IS ON

This induction cooktop is the perfect appliance for quick-meal artists, as it heats food fast—very fast! The surface stays cool to the touch.

Space Smarts

EVEN WITH THE BIGGEST kitchen, there never seems to be enough room for your stuff. There must be a gravitational force that attracts things to the kitchen, and then they stay, invited or uninvited. But don't fear—there's more space in your kitchen than you think.

You say your smaller kitchen cannot possibly expand. A day spent decluttering the cabinets may yield a few square inches, but that's not really much help. Getting rid of unnecessary casserole dishes or unused pots and pans is always a good idea, of course, but take a good long look inside your wall and base cabinets. Have you used them to their maximum effectiveness?

Start with the upper cabinets. Can you access all contents without a stepladder? When you visit the very top shelves, are you surprised at what you find? There is a whole new generation of cabinet inserts designed to maximize your inner space, while not interfering with your outer space, and that allow easy access to what lay inside. These can be a good investment in Right-Sizing your kitchen. Consider pull-down racks that function effortlessly to display the contents. In the process, you may weed out a bit more of the extras.

Another space to investigate in Right-Sizing your kitchen, is the crevice created when two cabinets don't meet perfectly. The little gap, or shortfall, between

SPICE ISLAND

Take advantage of lost space where the stove meets the cabinets, with shallow shelving for your favorite spices and usual seasonings.

base and wall cabinets can be used to store items you use often—spices, seasonings, or even a jar of rubber spatulas or whisks. A gap between lower cabinets is the perfect spot for frequently used trays or baking sheets.

When you have a look at your base cabinets, do you have to get down on your hands and knees to find pot lids or a rolling pin? Pullout drawers can help you avoid all that unnecessary crawling and hunting. One new trend in kitchen design is deeper drawers, instead of doors on base cabinets, making storage much easier.

Don't forget the corner cabinets. While a lazy Susan is one solution, it can waste up to 20 percent of the useable space, and contents sometimes slip off in the spin. Another idea is a swing-out, tiered shelving unit that brings the whole cabinet contents to you, instead of you having to reach inside.

The good news is that many of these new interior storage products can be retrofitted into existing cabinets, allowing you greater storing capability. The bad news is that they can't help you control your clutter. You're on your own with that! ●

USER-FRIENDLY

It's not just what's inside that counts, but how you reach it. Cleverly designed storage accessories such as this pullout rack makes the most of interior space.

Now It's Your Turn

Right-Sizing *Your* Kitchen

NOW IT'S TIME TO PAY ATTENTION TO YOUR KITCHEN. No matter the size, there never seems to be enough room for all your needs and wants. Smaller kitchens pose their own interesting design challenges, while larger ones present equally challenging obstacles to quality space and function. If you have already completed the "Cooking Style Audit" and "Kitchen Redesign Plan," your needs versus your wants should be clearer. Let's look at how to achieve the kitchen of your dreams within the space you have. ●

1. Open Shelves versus Wall Cabinets

THINK OPEN SHELVES ONLY

In a small kitchen or one with a lower ceiling, you may decide to eliminate wall cabinets. Use open shelves to create the illusion of more space. You will have easier access to the items stored there, but be aware: open shelving forces you to be more orderly.

RESULT:
Gain display space, lose storage

RETHINK WALL CABINETS

Where wall space is not so tight, rather than open shelves, consider replacing wall cabinet doors with glass-fronted doors, for display. If you have pantry items stored above the counter, however, keep them behind solid doors, unless you are very neat.

RESULT:
Gain display space and storage

2. Island versus Work Counter

THINK ISLAND ONLY

Even in a smaller kitchen there may be sufficient floor space to have an island. You'll need 30 inches on either side of the island, for passing space. To create an island workspace where you don't have room, consider a smaller, thinner, moveable unit you can use as needed. Store against a wall when not in use.

RESULT:
More workspace gained

THINK COUNTER ONLY

A peninsula addition will provide more working space, and more storage space beneath. For dual use, this could be designed as an eating bar. The peninsula should be at least 48 inches long, accommodate two barstools, and add sufficient workspace to justify the change.

RESULT:
Creates useage options

3. Hideaway versus Galley Kitchen

THINK BEHIND CLOSED DOORS

If your living space is totally open, you may want to disguise the kitchen by building around it, creating what looks like a series of 30-inch deep closets. Scaled-down appliances fit the closet depth. You'll sacrifice workspace, but a freestanding table can substitute. Doors close, kitchen disappears.

RESULT:
Hidden in a little extra space

THINK ONE-WALL KITCHEN

This is a good option for a smaller kitchen, an auxiliary one in a guest suite, or near a media room. Appliances and sink will be compact, and workspace will be at a premium unless you create space for working near this wall. If you are a heavy-duty cook, this option isn't for you.

RESULT:
Visible in existing space

4. More Storage

THINK WALL SPACE

Rather than expand into a closet to create a pantry, think about unused wall space. Replace your wall cabinets with taller ones. This may require getting rid of the soffits above the existing cabinets, which have a dated look anyway. The area above the existing cabinets should not be a dust-collecting, open space, but usable room for regularly used serving pieces.

RESULT:
More space added

RETHINK CABINETRY BENEATH SINK

New cabinet inserts will maximize the space of existing cabinets, with better organization of both drawers and door areas. It gives you easy access to frequently used items in the sink area. However, no food products should be stored here.

RESULT:
More function in same space

Where You Eat

Once upon a mealtime, *not so long ago, the family gathered around the dining room table. Sound like a fairy tale? Well, somewhere along the way we all got too busy, and now, so many time-challenged family members eat on the fly—and certainly not in the dining room!*

THE SEPARATE DINING ROOM CONCEPT HAS persisted, thanks to home builders and real estate agents who whisper "resale" into our ears. We know better. That room, used mostly for holiday meals, has become a space you walk through on the way to another room. Don't let this valuable, front-of-the-house real estate sit unloved and unused.

You probably aren't going to suddenly start having weekly dinner parties, or force your family to dine in that formal room every day, but take a good, long look at this underutilized room. It certainly could be put to better use than as a repository for uncomfortable furniture from another century! It could function as a home office, pool room, music space, a quiet place to read—or you *could* start having weekly dinner parties. It's time to reevaluate this room—and reinvent it—to suit your lifestyle.

If not in the dining room, where are you really eating your meals? How can you make that location better suited for the purpose? Does the kitchen counter or table serve as your out-the-door breakfast spot? Are the surfaces durable and easy to keep clean? Maybe the chairs need a new fabric, impervious to stains?

Of course no one eats in front of the TV, but just in case, are silverware and napkins handy in a nearby drawer? Can the coffee table handle one or more pizza boxes without you fussing? Do you have upholstery that camouflages soda spills?

Where at home do you eat dinner? The kitchen, the family room, breakfast area, or a random, makeshift spot? In all likelihood your answer is, "all of the above." Wherever it is, make this area a carefree, happy place for sharing a bite.

SET WITH STYLE

Not tucked away in a museum-like room, this table and chairs reflect the new, relaxed way to enjoy a meal together in a sunny room.

Eating Style Audit

Select the style that best reflects your and your family's eating habits. Then follow the tips below for creating more space and order suited to that style, during mealtimes.

ARE YOU A QUICK SNACKER?

O Need a place for "instant" meals
O Often use a coffee table as a dining surface
O Need space to assemble carry-out food onto plates

TIPS:

- Keep the place you eat most often near the kitchen
- Invest in a low-maintenance table and seating with easy-to-clean surfaces
- Keep a hand-held vacuum close by, for food spills
- Use a nearby cabinet or hutch to store plates and tableware for fast setup

ARE YOU A GREAT GOURMET?

O Want to show off your culinary creativity
O Desire simple, stylish surroundings
O Need flexible seating for added guests

TIPS:

- Use a neutral color palette in the dining area, to place focus on the meal
- The table should be sizeable enough to handle a large group, without crowding
- Keep a rolling cart handy for beverages, serving, and clearing
- Be creative and display finery on one wall of the dining area, instead of hiding it away

ARE YOU A LEISURELY DINER?

O Want a casual, inviting environment for friends and family
O Enjoy occasionally decorating the table
O Need a comfortable space to linger with family and guests

TIPS:

- Plan on a large serving surface for buffet-style presentation
- Organize china and glassware storage for stress-free access
- The table must accommodate eight or more *comfortable* chairs
- Create a warm atmosphere with dimmer-controlled lighting

ARE YOU AN EVERYDAY FEEDER?

O Need an easy-to-clean table and chairs
O Need your table to be multifunctional and sturdy
O Must have everyday items within reach

TIPS:

- Create a multifunctional eating area/homework and project station
- During breakfast, divide the eating area into a workspace and an eating space; pack lunches while the kids eat
- Place a "breakfast cabinet" stocked with cereals, spoons, and bowls, nearby
- Keep place-mats, napkins, and flatware convenient to the table

ARE YOU A REHEAT SPECIALIST?

O Need hassle-free food preparation
O Not particular about dining location
O Need to accommodate a changing number of diners

TIPS:

- Plan an eating area that doesn't require special care
- Keep a microwave, convection, or toaster oven close to where you eat
- Store dishes used for reheating near the prep area
- Keep extra chairs handy for a full house
- Put up a bulletin board and have family members post updates

Great Gourmet
That's Entertainment

GRAPE EXPECTATIONS

By turning your old dining room into a wine cave, you can create a very enjoyable, new eating space, with a gourmet twist.

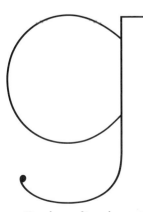

OOD LIVING AND good eating certainly go hand in hand. Despite today's accelerated lifestyles, a quick glance at the many cooking magazines on the corner newsstand confirms the continued appeal of an exquisite meal, served in beautiful surroundings.

Simply reading the recipes in any one of these magazines conjures heavenly flavors, and provides inspiration for special gatherings—not to mention your stash of heavily annotated, finger-smudged cookbooks and recipes that still motivate your culinary efforts.

Admittedly, with so much going on in your life, entertaining has taken a back seat. There was a time when you hosted dinners with greater frequency. Even though you hold fewer gatherings, you still prepare for them, much as a general gets ready for war. After all, you do have your Great Gourmet status to uphold, and you cannot let standards slip in these trying times!

"Foodie literature" has informed your cooking style over the years, so the challenge for you is not the food and beverages, but the setting for your dinner party. The old dining room seems so tired and stodgy, and no longer

POLISHED PERFORMER

These days, anything goes in any eating space. Tuck a polished stone sink and elegant faucet into a buffet, for ease and convenience.

fits your style. Besides, that room is probably now a library, which *may* still work for that cozy, holiday soirée you're planning.

You tend toward the formal, but nowadays you prefer your parties to be relatively stress-free and slightly more casual. How about drinks in the kitchen, or a nearby place to settle in that invites conversation, as you perform your magic at the oversized range? Should everyone gather at a big round table, or how about two or three smaller tables for four? Maybe a long, skinny table with seating on one side, looking right into that gourmet kitchen?

If the table sets the tone, your attitude is definitely 21st century. The surface is matte, not polished, because your meticulously-prepared meal is going to be the star of the evening.

In supporting roles, literally as well as figuratively, are your chairs. Nothing says, "welcome to my home," better than comfortable seating—especially at the dining table. Make sure they're not *too* soft, or too big to fit around the table.

Storage of your finery should be convenient, and the style options are endless. Determine how much space you really need for tableware, serving pieces, and linens before you purchase any cabinetry. This may apply to wine storage as well. Once you have an inventory, find a cabinet that accommodates your tableware, and enhances your space and décor.

Get ready, get set, entertain! ●

Eating Redesign Plan

Before you start planning to change your eating space, look at the lists below. The items you check should help guide you in assessing your space, and how it might work best for you. Use these responses to define the problems, as well as the solutions.

Reasons for making a change?
(check all that apply)
- Entire eating area is too small
- Table cannot expand to meet needs
- Table is out of date
- Layout is not functional
- Lack of storage for china, glassware, and supplies
- Chairs are unappealing or uncomfortable
- Poor lighting
- Not enough serving space
- Inadequate electrical outlets
- Nearby distractions, such as the TV

Who uses this room?
(check all that apply)
- Adults
- Older adults
- Children
- Other family members
- Guests

How is it used?
(check all that apply)
- Eating
- Working
- Doing homework
- Snacking
- Reading e-mail
- Writing
- Extension of the kitchen

What do you need to store here?
(check all that apply)
- China
- Glassware
- Flatware
- Serving platters
- Table linens and napkins
- Trays
- Wine
- Water and other beverages
- Cereals, snacks, cookies

What do you need for more comfort?
(check all that apply)
- Better/comfortable table and chairs
- More storage space
- Improved lighting
- Low-maintenance flooring or rug
- Additional serving space
- Innovative way to expand the table
- Adequate room
- Less furniture
- More furniture
- Electrical outlets for small appliances and computers
- Easy-to-clean surfaces
- Cart for transporting to and from the kitchen

Trade-Offs

As you map out a plan for Right-Sizing your eating space, think about the trade-offs below. Remember to take into consideration the amount of space you really have, while weighing wants versus needs.

VERSUS

Dedicated Eating Area ←→ **Moveable Eating Setup**
More workspace / Flexible space

Rectangular Table ←→ **Round Table**
Conventional seating / More informal seating

Square Table ←→ **Round Table**
No head-of-table position / Promotes conversation

Bar-Height Table ←→ **Conventional-Height Table**
Requires barstools or chairs / Uses existing chairs

Rolling Chair ←→ **Static Chair**
More mobility / Less mobility

VERSUS

Built-In Seating ←→ **Freestanding Chairs**
Inflexible; uses less space / Flexible; uses more space

Snack Storage Cabinet ←→ **Standard Kitchen Storage**
Immediate access / Less accessible

Nearby Serving Space ←→ **Kitchen Counter**
Closer to eating site / Possibly less convenient

China Storage Unit ←→ **Kitchen Cabinet Storage**
Convenient to table / Less handy

THE ART OF EATING

Have fun with your eating area by mixing furniture styles and materials. A dark finish makes the look much more casual.

Everyday Feeder
Café Style

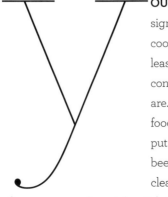

OU PROBABLY NEVER signed up to be a short-order cook, but let's face it—at least where your family is concerned, that's what you are. Plus, you shop for the food, you unpack it, you put it away, and after it's been cooked and eaten, you cleanup. Every now and then, someone else might pitch in and clear the table, but mostly you are "it." You are an Everyday Feeder.

Yes, you do have other things to do in your life, but when breakfast or supper comes along, you change into your virtual apron and get busy. The key is an eating area located near the kitchen, keeping the hungry masses from getting underfoot while you prepare the meal.

A sturdy table and chairs with durable surfaces are crucial to an active family. Spills and accidents are bound to happen, so this is not the place for a highly polished table or chintz-covered chair cushions. What you need is an almost indestructible, laminate-type surface, and robust fabrics that are impervious to stains or smudges— even from the dog or cat.

Not enough room for a table and chairs? A counter with barstools is the next best solution. Measure the height of the counter (or table) to ensure a perfect fit. To sit comfortably, allow 10 to 12 inches between the top of the seat and the bottom of the eating surface. You will need between 25 and 30 inches from the center of one stool, to the next. To determine how many stools you can fit at the counter, divide its length (in inches) by 28, and that's how many stools will fit!

Flooring must be easy to mop and vacuum. If you decide you'd like a rug for the area, think low-maintenance. Indoor-outdoor rugs are available in many fashionable colors and sizes. They can look great, and best of all, they can practically be hosed off in case of major disasters.

If you have room near your eating area for a small cabinet, you can keep cereals, breads, snacks, and maybe even the toaster or toaster oven close at hand. Call it your breakfast bar. It conveniently places most needs for the first meal of the day, and maybe the last nosh of the evening, right near the eating area. Others can help themselves, and it reduces the need for you to be on constant call! ●

HIGH CHAIR

Barstools are like magnets in an eat-in kitchen. Make sure they're comfortable, and allow enough space to spread out.

ORDER KEEPER

In a small kitchen, a hutch can provide much-needed extra storage; or turn it into a breakfast bar with all the fixings for a quick meal.

Quick Snacker

Ringside Seats

OES IT SEEM AS IF YOU never have time for lavish meals these days? Perhaps the best you can muster is the creative reassembly of ready-to-serve foods? Maybe you carry-in the main ingredient—say, barbecued chicken—with the hope the rest will fall into place from whatever you have on hand in the pantry, fridge, or freezer? Better yet, you pick up the phone and order a complete meal, to be delivered in less time than it would take to cook it! If all this sounds familiar, you are a Quick Snacker.

How did this happen? When the walls of the kitchen came tumbling down, what used to be the breakfast room became the new eating arena—and everyone wants to be near the action. The cook needs to be at the center of the serving area (even if she or he just ordered food in), and the table and chairs now free-float to adjust to the view—which may be out the window or onto the

AROUND THE TABLE
Even if you snack, sit with ease around this hassle-free round table. Slipcover your chairs for easier maintenance.

SPACE CRAFT

Extend your storage beyond the actual kitchen with well-placed cabinets that act as a buffet. Add lighting for more drama.

kitchen and the cook. No escaping your hungry audience!

If a varied selection of hors d'oeuvres and crispy breads is your idea of good meal, so be it. However, you really must set a table, albeit a relaxed one, so you and your guests or family can enjoy the hassle-free meal. Lay it out for all to enjoy, maybe on a round table, making it easy to see the offerings while promoting better conversation. Forget that head-of-the-table concept—a round table puts everyone on equal footing.

Even more important are the chairs, which should invite friends and family to linger. Don't be shy about the "bottom test" before buying your chairs. Take the time to sit for awhile and seriously evaluate their comfort level. Also, remember chairs should be easy to push away from the table after eating. Allow about 30 inches behind all the chairs, for passage as well as push-back.

Now is the time to admit you sometimes eat in front of the TV. No big surprise, since easy-to-serve/easy-to-eat pizza and Chinese food are tasty staples of our evening menus these days. In this situation, a cocktail or coffee table that's high enough to serve from, or more likely, to eat from, is important. There are some that actually adjust to a perfect height for dining—during your favorite reality show.

Your organized snack-fests will leave you feeling less stressed and unhurried—not to mention your reputation as the best snack cook in the neighborhood will remain unchallenged! ●

EXPANDABLE OPTION

Who's going to know that you eat by the TV? The evidence is hidden with this lift-up coffee table that disguises itself.

parental peace, not to mention facilitate easy cleanup.

As children grow up, the dining table can be a place to learn manners, learn about new foods, and maybe even how to entertain. This is the place they will bring friends for after-school snacks, and—sooner than you know—for late-night bites as well.

Making room for everyone is often a test; the number of people who gather around can multiply exponentially. What to do? Banquettes tend *not* to work very well. As great as they look, the fixed seating space leaves little or no opportunity to expand. That said, they can be the perfect solution for small, tight areas; a trade-off worth considering when you prepare a seating plan. The same tricky problem happens around eating islands. A few barstools may fit well, but leave no room for a drop-in, who is left standing or leaning. And while it may be fun to sit on barstools, they can be safety hazards, especially for smaller children. If you do opt for stools, make sure they are sturdy and not easily tipped over during spontaneous roughhousing. Also, consider stools with backs to greatly increase your comfort factor.

Enjoy eating in safety, style, and hopefully all together. ●

Kid Smarts

GETTING EVERYONE TO THE TABLE SOMETIMES feels like a challenge even contestants on *Survivor* could never overcome. Everyone sitting down together, typical of 1950s sitcoms, just doesn't happen today, with late football practice, can't-miss school events, or maybe Mom is still in her office.

But put a favorite dish on the table, and magically reluctant family members come running! It's pretty special when you do sit down together. And if you really think about it, memories of the family table are part of what we savor most about our childhood.

Actually, the family table takes a lot of abuse through the years. Younger children, who have graduated from a high chair to their own place at the table, still have a tendency to spill. Avoid high-maintenance finishes, opting for durable surfaces. This will help keep

FAMILY TIME

Sitting on a barstool at the counter makes mealtime more fun. Make sure the stool is sturdy and easy to reach for small legs.

NESTLE IN

Create a banquette effect with a knee or half wall, and a well-cushioned cabinet to sit on.

Measuring Up
Eating Dimension Guide

How you Right-Size your eating environment, depends chiefly on your choice and arrangement of the table and chairs. The drawings below show several table and seating options, with minimum (MIN) and recommended (REC) values, for comfort and usability.

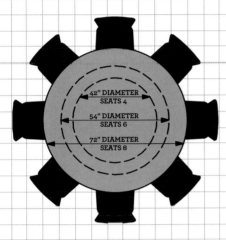

42" DIAMETER
SEATS 4

54" DIAMETER
SEATS 6

72" DIAMETER
SEATS 8

ROUND TABLES

36" x 48"
SEATS 4

36" x 60"
SEATS 6

36" x 78"
SEATS 8

30" MIN
36" REC

RECTANGULAR TABLES

GENERAL TIPS:

- Round tables look best in square rooms
- A large round or square table invites lively conversation
- Smaller square tables add versatility and intimacy; use two or three rather than a single large one, especially if the eating space has multiple functions
- Pedestal bases make adding extra chairs easier—leg bases lend more support

- Though 30 inches is the minimum clearance between chair and wall (or furniture), 36 inches eliminates the "squeeze"
- Sturdy shouldn't mean uncomfortable; add a seat cushion if chairs are not upholstered
- Upholstered folding chairs are perfect for additional seating at large gatherings
- Place a cabinet near the table, for handy storage of everyday items
- For easy care, use indoor/outdoor carpeting under the family table
- Lighting should always be dimmer-controlled

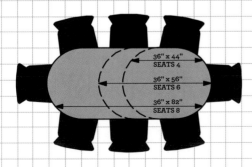

36" x 44"
SEATS 4

36" x 56"
SEATS 6

36" x 82"
SEATS 8

OVAL TABLES

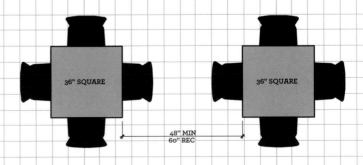

36" SQUARE

36" SQUARE

48" MIN
60" REC

SQUARE TABLES

DINING CLUB

Eat in style with these iconic, Eames chairs that fit quite nicely into almost any dining space, even the kitchen.

Leisurely Diner

Set With Style

HE DINING ROOM MAY SIT EMPTY most of the time, but there is a recent trend toward a kind of semiformal gathering in this place. Maybe you've already settled into a more casual arrangement, closer to the kitchen. But if you're thinking that with some serious changes, the dining room can sparkle again, and if you're ready to polish up the silver and dust off the good china, you're part of the new breed of Leisurely Diner.

Your entertaining style and eating habits today are not your mother's and are certainly a long way from your grandmother's. Surely you'd rather forget the invisible velvet ropes that said this space was "off limits," and those incredibly hard chairs you sat on, for what felt like hours.

If your objective is to have an "elbows on the table" place to eat, it's time to get creative. Banish that high-maintenance table to another place or person, through eBay, a tag sale, resale, etc. Find a more casual, comfortable table and chairs, to reflect the perfectly at ease style you want.

Don't feel constrained; everything doesn't have to match perfectly. A refreshing new-old idea is to incorporate a bench or upholstered settee on one side of the table. It adds drama and is convenient as well. If your table is round, there is curved seating available, making the dining experience unique.

Storage cabinets for china, glassware, flatware, and linens are back in style. They are a necessary ingredient for easier entertaining. Forget about that old breakfront or china cabinet (it could move on, along with the table). You need something packed with style—a painted, "almost antique" hutch, or built-in cabinets with an accent color inside. Avoid having to dig out what you need from the very top of your kitchen cabinets, or from the back of that gaping, bottom corner cabinet.

SHOWING OFF

Give your good china a new home in an almost pantry-like setting. Use a series of custom cabinets, with detailed moldings, to create a furniture effect.

GATHER 'ROUND

For a special effect, choose a curved, upholstered bench for your round dining table. It complements the table shape.

Don't forget about logistics either. How far do you have to go to serve your meal? Then consider how far the return trip is. If it's a bit of a hike, a stylish cart can multitask the bringing and removing of food, wine, plates, and glassware. However, remember you need a convenient place to store it. Carts can be a blessing or a curse.

The whole point is to create a comfortable eating space, so family and friends will want to linger at the table, laughing and chatting when the meal is through.

Push back, lean back. You're the host with the most! ●

Reheat Specialist
Self-Service

SEATING PLAN

Install a large counter to use as a convenient place to perch, while you enjoy that delicious meal you just warmed up.

YOUR LIFESTYLE doesn't include a lot of cooking, does it? The problem with an over-scheduled life is that it leaves little time to even *think* about putting meals together. There may have been a time when you found relaxation in cooking, but today you would rather go to the gym to unwind. Besides, you can barely keep on top of all your other obligations and responsibilities. This is how you became a Reheat Specialist.

You are not alone in this regard. There are many who start out the day with good intentions of turning out a nourishing evening meal. But, when you stumble in at the end of a long day, you have neither the time nor the energy to start cooking. Life is all about trade-offs, and luckily, you can reheat leftovers. Try calling them "planned-overs"—it doesn't sound quite as bad!

What you really need is a refreshing drink, and someone, or something, else do your cooking. Your best ally, in this case, is your microwave or speed oven. It should be close to your eating area, though not necessarily in the kitchen. You're tired and every step, at this point, delays putting food on the table. Maybe you transfer the food onto a plate, or just eat it from one of those combination storage/microwaveable containers.

Speaking of these containers, a good way for the

Reheat Specialist to keep things simple and stress-free is to organize a handy, dedicated storage space. Instead of stuffing these dishes, containers, and utensils into an out-of-the-way spot above the refrigerator, gather them in one spot near the microwave or oven. Another idea: clear out that buffet filled with Grandma's china (that you never use), and replace those pieces with what you really do use!

Of course, *where* you eat should be hassle-free as well. At the counter in the kitchen? Maybe the little banquette in the corner? You might possibly flop down in front of the TV to watch the news, with a tray of food on your lap. If you work at home, your work surface may do double-duty as a dining table. Wherever your arrangement, you want cozy and comfortable, without a care as to where you put down your drink. This is no time to waste time. Enjoy it while it's hot! ●

MAKE IT WORK

Who's to know this beautiful combination of glass-topped tables were selected because they were just pizza-box size? Better than your lap!

DOUBLE DUTY

Most of the time this glass-topped surface is your desk, but when friends come over, you can convert it easily into a dining table.

4

Space Smarts

HOSPITALITY MEANS MAKING SURE YOU
always have room at your table for one more. Suddenly
having an extra guest, with no room at the table to
squeeze them in, is one of life's more embarrassing
moments. Don't wait for that moment to decide on a
creative solution to this potentially awkward situation.
Here are just a few ideas for bringing guests to your table.

While you may normally have only four to six diners
at your table, the holidays require a more expansive
seating arrangement. Many dining tables come with an
extra leaf or two, but where are they? Stuck in the back
of a closet you have to empty in order to find them? Look
into the latest generation of dining tables. Their leaves
are built right in, making the task of enlarging the table
effortless. Simply pull a little lever and the leaf pops up.
No storage necessary.

There are also tables that can change shape, from
square to round by flipping up hidden drop leaves.
Another style, perfectly round, becomes a long oval.
Keep in mind, you can always rent large, round tops
to be secured to your own tables. If you are really in a
pinch, rent several tables, the linens to match, and folding

TURNING TABLES

*Don't worry about
storing your table's
leaves. The latest
tables have handy
self-store capacity.*

PARTY TRICKS

*Not only does
this table rise
and lower, but
it holds dishes
underneath, too.*

chairs. Catering and party suppliers have just what you
need for that big, once-a-year party.

No room for a dining table? There is actually a sofa
console available that opens up, or flips out, into a long,
thin dining table. You may not be able to get a cast of
thousands around this table, but it could serve as a perfect
eating area for four to six good friends.

If you cannot even imagine having a sit-down dinner in
your home, how about a buffet? Nowadays there are clever,
adjustable tables that can be raised to 40 or 42 inches, a
perfect height for a buffet, serving up your best lap food.
Just make sure you have enough chairs. ●

Now It's Your Turn

Right-Sizing *Your* Eating Area

W**HETHER YOU HAVE REINVENTED THE EXISTING** dining room, or are rethinking your family eating spaces, you need to create a layout that fits your eating style. Refer to your results from the "Eating Style Audit," "Eating Area Redesign Plan," and the "Dimensions Guide." Look at how much space you have, and how much you need to fulfill your plans. The goal is to make the eating space more functional and less cluttered—wherever you eat. ●

Dedicated Eating Table versus Multitasking Table

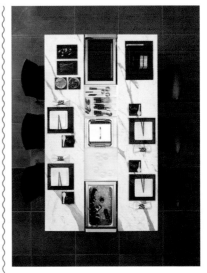

THINK MULTITASKING

● *From casual lunches to formal dinners, to homework sessions, choose an all-purpose table that works hard for you. Consider casters, so it can be repositioned when working or entertaining. This alternative gives you flexibility in layout, as circumstances dictate.*

RESULT:
Allows more flexible space

RETHINK DEDICATED

● *Consider changing the shape of your table. A taller one can be a slimmer, more dramatic choice. Also, think about how many people you need to fit around it—a round table can accommodate more. Be certain it fits through the door before you buy.*

RESULT:
More features in same space

THINK UNCONVENTIONAL

● *In Europe and Asia, the rage is a table with cooking capabilities. By including a grill you encourage more sociable meals in a larger, rectangular space. Since this tends to dominate any room, be clear about what you may be trading-off in the process.*

RESULT:
More space needed

Where You Relax

Who really has the time to relax? *Maybe you prefer to think of relaxation as crashing, cuddling, remote controlling, crafting, or chatting. This means that in our time-challenged lives, we still have a choice of what to do during those down times, when nothing else is planned!*

SHOULD YOU SLIP INTO SOMETHING COMFORTABLE, flop on the couch, and zone out? Perhaps you would like to nestle up close to a loved one (maybe the family pet), and read? Another alternative is to reach for the TV remote, and immerse yourself in a movie or favorite program. You might sneak away for a couple of hours of comforting craftwork. Last but not least, how about a catch-up with one or more family members, without distraction?

Where you relax is a whole other topic. It's certainly not in the living room, unless you had the foresight to really "live" there instead of just walking through it. After all, it may be more like a museum, filled with Grandma's formal furniture, designed for use in the previous century.

Most of us now elect to use the family room, previously known as the den, study, rumpus room, great room, etc. The enticing sofas or sectional, comfy recliners, or overstuffed chairs promise the right environment for putting up your feet. Then again, if this room is fairly large and not a snug space for just one or two people, maybe the bedroom has become your new living room. That soft chaise or heavenly bed now competes for your attention with the family room furniture. Just ask the dog, the flop-master of comfort. He or she has tested them all when you weren't looking.

If where you relax doesn't meet your requirements, it's time to Right-Size the space to make it function better for you and family members. Soon you'll be able to plunk down into a serene space, with perfectly controlled lighting, well-placed tables to hold that soothing cup of coffee or tea, and a soft rug or carpet underfoot to thrill your bare toes.

Then all you have to do is crash, cuddle, control, craft, or yes, even chat.

COMFORT ZONE

Any room can be made right for relaxing. You need really comfortable seating, a great flat screen TV, and a background that creates a lovely environment.

Relaxing Style Audit

Select the style that best reflects your favorite way to relax. Then follow the tips below to help you find true tranquility, suited to that style.

ARE YOU AN AVID READER?

- ○ Your nose is in a book whenever you have time
- ○ Frequently find yourself in bookstores
- ○ Lose all sense of time when reading

TIPS:

- Organize dust-collecting stacks of books onto shelves; arrange by title, author, and/or topic for easier access
- Make use of "found" spaces; shallow bookcases work well in hallways, stair landings, under stairs, and otherwise awkward corners
- Plan on seating with good, firm support for longer reading sessions
- Make sure your reading space has adequate light, originating over your shoulder, without glare
- Eliminate rummaging by reserving a special place for current reading materials, in a multiuser space

ARE YOU A SWEET TALKER?

- ○ Love to keep up with family activities and decisions
- ○ Find it easier to express yourself by talking than writing
- ○ People tend to turn to you for advice and counsel

TIPS:

- Create one or more areas in your home for serious discussions
- Casual chats with friends are best at the kitchen table
- Avoid distractions; pull shades to block sun or glare; play soft music for a serene mood, but turn off the TV
- Allow 19 to 24 inches between chairs; the same measurements apply to a couch; sitting too close can hinder conversation.
- Opt for a round or square table; they are more conducive to discussion, as there is no head of table

ARE YOU A CONSUMMATE CRAFTER?

- ○ Feel passionate about anything handmade
- ○ Enjoy working with your hands
- ○ Find creative work very relaxing

TIPS:

- Keep supplies in plastic boxes and label the contents; periodically weed out duplicates or out-of-date items
- Allow enough workspace to spread out; use surfaces suitable for cutting or gluing, as well as easy cleaning
- Designate space for project storage; use dowels for hanging fabric or canvas, and easels for display or drying
- Reserve an area for works-in-progress; make sure the space can't be disturbed by family traffic or curious pets

ARE YOU A MOVIE FAN?

- ○ Turn to movie review section of newspapers or magazines first
- ○ Always have popcorn ready in your pantry
- ○ Subscribe to movie networks, Netflix, Red Door Movies, etc.

TIPS:

- Choose one area for DVD storage, even if you watch movies in several locations; a well-organized DVD library means easy access
- Natural light control is important to enjoyment; darken the room with blackout shades, blinds, or other appropriate window coverings
- Illuminate a path to the exit(s), with night lights plugged into wall outlets
- Chairs or sofas with a slight recline provide good neck and back support; if you have back problems, straight-backed chairs are a better option; if watching in bed, use pillows for leg, head, and back support

ARE YOU A COUCH POTATO?

- ○ Your sofa is the center of after-work or weekend activities
- ○ The TV remote sits primarily by your seat
- ○ You wish your lamp table was really a small refrigerator

TIPS:

- To accommodate a recliner, measure upright dimensions of the chair for delivery, and fully extended length for placement
- Space-saver recliners can be placed closer to walls
- Elevate your feet using a small ottoman on casters, with hidden storage capability
- Sectionals work well in shared spaces, and are designed to be rearranged; make sure it fits through your door openings
- Lighting, whether table lamps, floor lamps, or ceiling lights, should be on dimmers to enhance media viewing

Sweet Talker
Chat Room

EXTING YOUR THOUGHTS WILL never replace a good conversation. It certainly isn't as satisfying, even if you do get a speedy reply from the respondent. Somehow, having a good talk really requires two people and a period of precious, undisturbed time. But do you ever have enough time to chat with those you love or care about? The television is distracting, the phone rings off the hook, the computer is compelling, or there are other chores that have to be done before going to bed. It's not always a matter of time, but sometimes of place. Where can you go to find a quiet, inviting place, without interruptions?

It may be just a corner of an otherwise occupied room, or perhaps even the luxury of a space you have to yourselves. All you need are two cozy, well-padded chairs, or a comfy couch large enough for two. Maybe a fireplace or soft lighting, and some background music would set the mood for talking. A little wine or a good cup of coffee can also fuel good conversation.

Many great conversations have been had around the kitchen table. Of course the family room, after the kids have gone to sleep, may be a good choice because of that big sectional or sofa, where you can flop down together. If your bedroom is large enough to include a pair of cushy chairs or chaises, then it might be the go-to place for some chitchat.

CONVERSATION PIECE

Create the perfect room for talking, by adding color and comfort. Make sure the room has enough seating space for two, and the option of providing privacy if needed.

TABLE TALK

An end table always makes a good resting spot for your favorite beverage. Keep the height difference between the tabletop and sofa (or chair) arm to within one foot, so no one has to stretch.

MUSIC STORE

While a TV may be distracting, having some soft music in the background adds to a relaxing conversation. It can soothe a heated debate, or warm a cool talk.

As an alternate idea, head to that unused living room. It's probably the most readily available room in the house, especially if you don't use it all that much—except for state occasions or holiday celebrations. Also, it's probably the quietest and has all the ingredients for a good chat—separation from household traffic or distractions; comfortable, largely unused furniture; soft lighting; and perhaps even a door you can close.

Maybe it's time to turn the living room into a more usable space you can enjoy. If this is a part of the house that has been too-long ignored, take another look at the term "living room," and decide to actually live there! It's a great place for a chat, but surely you can make better use of this valuable real estate, than to hold up the front of the house.

In the end, what you need, wherever you have your heart-to-heart, is space for two comfortable chairs. You need a minimum of 18 to 24 inches between chairs. If your choice is a sofa, allow two feet per person for comfort. Much of this depends upon the level of intimacy between you and the other person, of course. Do you feel comfortable sitting close to each other? How close is too close? Being a Sweet Talker, those are questions you can easily answer. ●

Relaxing Redesign Plan

Before you start planning to change the areas you and your family use to relax, look at the lists below. The items you check should help guide you in assessing your space, and how it might work best for you. Use these responses to define the problems, as well as the solutions.

Reasons for making a change?
(check all that apply)
- ○ Room is too small
- ○ Need a quiet space
- ○ Poor seating arrangement
- ○ Need lighting control
- ○ More natural light options
- ○ Uncomfortable chairs
- ○ Noise
- ○ Inadequate seating
- ○ Worn flooring
- ○ Sofa needs replacing
- ○ Need space to craft
- ○ New flat screen TV
- ○ No room for eating

Who uses this room?
(check all that apply)
- ○ Adults
- ○ Older adults
- ○ Children
- ○ Guests
- ○ Pets

How is it used?
(check all that apply)
- ○ Watching TV
- ○ Watching movies/DVDs
- ○ Entertaining
- ○ Eating casual meals
- ○ Crafting
- ○ Talking
- ○ Homework
- ○ Playing video (or other) games
- ○ Computer activities
- ○ Reading
- ○ Listening to music
- ○ Napping

What do you need to store here?
(check all that apply)
- ○ TV
- ○ Sound equipment
- ○ CDs/DVDs
- ○ Reading materials
- ○ Games
- ○ Electronics supplies
- ○ Speakers
- ○ Photo albums
- ○ Computer equipment
- ○ Craft supplies
- ○ Pet toys

What do you need for more comfort?
(check all that apply)
- ○ Adequate seating space
- ○ More storage space
- ○ More workspace
- ○ Better task and/or ambient lighting
- ○ Control of natural light
- ○ Good traffic flow
- ○ Rug or carpeting
- ○ Room for reclining
- ○ Flexible seating for family and guests
- ○ Dedicated single-function space
- ○ Sound control
- ○ Easy-clean fabrics

Trade-Offs

As you map out a plan for Right-Sizing the spaces where you most like to relax, think about the trade-offs below. Remember to take into consideration the amount of space you really have, while weighing wants versus needs.

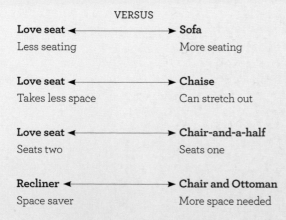

VERSUS

Love seat ←——→ **Sofa**
Less seating / More seating

Love seat ←——→ **Chaise**
Takes less space / Can stretch out

Love seat ←——→ **Chair-and-a-half**
Seats two / Seats one

Recliner ←——→ **Chair and Ottoman**
Space saver / More space needed

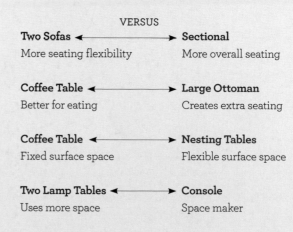

VERSUS

Two Sofas ←——→ **Sectional**
More seating flexibility / More overall seating

Coffee Table ←——→ **Large Ottoman**
Better for eating / Creates extra seating

Coffee Table ←——→ **Nesting Tables**
Fixed surface space / Flexible surface space

Two Lamp Tables ←——→ **Console**
Uses more space / Space maker

5

DOUBLE FEATURE

Arrange an intimate media room in a large space, by using a sectional to define the viewing area. The couch creates a room within a room.

Movie Fan

A Moving Experience

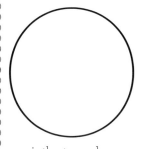

NCE UPON A TIME, NOT so long ago, you piled into the car with family and friends, and headed to the movies for thrills, chills, and excitement. But now, your flat screen TV has replaced the large screen at the movie theater, and your sound system makes those special effect explosions more stimulating than ever. This is what you look forward to, at the end of a rough week or dreadful day: Fantasyland in dazzling high-definition, blazing color, and digital surround sound, right in your own home!

This may be difficult to explain to someone who's not the true Movie Fan you are, but once they've shared the experience with you, you'll have a friend for life. After all, the TV used to sit like an uninvited guest in the corner of your family room. Maybe you actually tried to hide that blank, grey screen behind the closed doors of some attractive cupboard. Now, with slim flat screens taking over the market, stylish integration into the room where you relax is not only possible, but also inspiring.

Whether wall mounted or located on a low-lying console or table, the screen must be at an appropriate viewing height when you are seated. Along with a well-placed sofa, easy chairs that swivel prevent twisting or straining (like a horror film effect) to see the screen.

The same principle applies if you're installing the TV in your bedroom. If watching from bed, be sure to keep in mind the height of your mattress, plus the "height" of your feet, to get a good idea of where to place the screen. You want to be able to see over your toes!

Even if you're planning a wall mount, you'll still need appropriate cabinetry for storing all your DVDs and equipment, either underneath or nearby. There's also wire management for the DVD or Blu-ray player, satellite or cable box, and other cables to consider. Obviously, you'll want this television unit to blend into your existing décor, so a silver/grey frame may seem a bit less conspicuous than a black one. You may decide to faintly disguise it with a custom frame or special glass.

DIGITAL DECOR

Don't be afraid to move your new slim TV into your main sitting area. Simply rest it on an elegant cabinet that can hold all the accessories.

ARMCHAIR THEATER

Sit back and really enjoy the film's special effects in these recliners. They are as cool as the science fiction you're watching.

Comfortable seating, with back and leg support, is very important when you settle in to watch a double feature. If you're in the market, test out a few chairs. Learn to recognize the features that make the chair feel agreeable to you. Is the padding too hard, too soft, or just right? Make sure the chair fits your particular body type; for example, you may want a deeper seat if you are long-legged. The height of the arms, the pitch of the back, and the support under your knees should feel just right. Follow the same principles when purchasing a sofa.

Finally, remember you need control over the spill of natural light, as well as the interior lighting. Will the windows reflect in the screen at night? Certainly a well-darkened room enhances viewing quality, and one solution is blackout shades. But draperies, blinds, or a combination of window treatments, can be installed to get the same darkening effect.

So now, everything ready? Popcorn popped? Sit back, dim the lights, and...ACTION! ●

5

Avid Reader

One for the Books

WHO SAID THAT books are so yesterday? Certainly not someone who loves the heft of a book in their hands, and nothing more than the pleasure of being transported by the written word. For an Avid Reader, the sheer act of reading slows down your life, and the cares of the day recede as you head deeper into your book.

The key ingredient for an Avid Reader—after a good book, of course—is the perfect chair. There is some controversy over whether a slight tilt-back in the chair is better than the straight back of many so-called "reading

chairs." This is a matter of personal comfort, of course. The chair should be commodious, and cause no strain to your neck and back.

The supporting role in this relaxing activity is a good lamp to provide adequate illumination for the book. Three-way bulbs are the accepted norm, so the lamp and chair can be used for other purposes. Do avoid glare from a poorly placed lamp, or squinting from insufficient wattage. It can make or break your reading experience.

A well-proportioned side table for the lamp (or combination lamp-table), your book, beverage, and any collateral material is important. The height of this table should be just about parallel to the height of the chair's arm, making for easy transfers.

But Right-Sizing comprises more than seating and

LIGHT READING

Part of relaxing and quiet reading is having great control over your lighting. Install dimmers on your lamps or in wall switches, for just the right level of ambient illumination, and a serene atmosphere.

lighting concerns. Depending on your level of attention, and tolerance for other distractions such as music or other noise, your surrounding space requirements are equally important.

What happens when you cannot—or will not—part with your books? With overflowing shelves or stacks on the floor, you're surrounded by clutter! You need books for inspiration, you say, for instruction, or for re-reading. Everyone tells you to weed them out, but it really *is* difficult to part with these friends, and they do accumulate over time. The secret is that you can—and will—reduce your stash when you must. Besides, the process will keep you in touch with your collection.

Start by making a pile of your softcover books; they are of less value, and can be easily found or borrowed later. Next, make a pile of long-ignored volumes from school, or those you haven't thought about in years. Lastly, pile up your favorites. Carefully sort through the lot, and be honest with yourself. Hopefully, you'll have a stack, or two or three, to donate to the thrift shop. As for the nice mound of books you simply *must* keep, organize and store them on shelves, instead of in nooks and crannies throughout your home. If space is really an issue, make good use of a hallway by lining it with shallow shelves on one side. It can add character and color to a long narrow space.

Of course, there are Avid Readers who have moved away from print, and enjoy their written adventures via the Kindle and other eReader devices. These users may find it easier to surrender even their most-loved books, which are probably available for download, along with textbooks and newspapers.

Whether you deal with tome or technology, you will have increased your storage area and created a serene, inviting space, in which you can relax, unwind, and read.

Now, pull up that chair, turn on the light—maybe some music too—and get back to that book. ●

REAR VIEW

If you are planning on floating a chair in the room, consider the design of the back, since you will approach it from that side. Remember— always have perfect support, whether seated on a chair or sofa.

SWITCHED ON

Wherever you read, make sure the light source is over your shoulder, and the page is illuminated without eye-straining glare.

Kid Smarts

CHILDREN TODAY HAVE THE ADVANTAGE OF state-of-the-art electronics, but they still work hard at learning—no doubt mastering technology more quickly than you do now. Still, after a long, hard day at school, they want to relax, just like you.

This might, of course, take a slightly different tack, but they still need to cuddle, chat, craft, control, or crash like adults. They want a hug or a kiss from a parent (depending on their age), and certainly a little chitchat about what they did that day. While older kids may head to their video games or computers, the little ones still love their easels and hands-on projects. Certainly, stretching out on the couch, watching cartoons, is a favorite late afternoon pastime.

Many children's activities need age-appropriate furniture, or space on the floor to spread out and play. Ideally, these activities can be restricted to their room, or in (or near) the kitchen, where surfaces are more forgiving than the family room carpet or couch.

Creating a special play area may encourage their exuberance and protect your décor. A space designed to let them "work" or play, with room to store supplies, may be located in a corner of the family room, or maybe

PLAYTIME

Learning your ABCs can certainly be a playful activity. Start your child early with a sturdy little wooden table and chair to support those building blocks of language.

CRAFT WORK

Keep the bits and pieces of your child's art projects contained with kid-sized shelving and craft storage units.

in their bedroom. Do a little preliminary thinking about childproofing the space, as well as the required maintenance and protection of nearby surfaces.

Open floor space is essential for kids of all ages. Kids love to spread out, but be mindful of sharp corners of tables, chairs, or even doors. This rule does not just apply to the littlest members of the family; accidents happen at all ages when we least expect it. Beanbag chairs or oversized floor pillows are good alternatives, and make inviting seating or lounging.

A child-sized table and chairs is terrifically inviting to little ones. Small-scale "easy chairs" make for comfy cartoon watching, and these kinds of pieces come with easy-care finishes and fabrics. If you don't have scaled-down furniture to fit the littlest members of your family, washable slipcovers for regular-scale pieces is a must. This is especially true of recliners. It's difficult to keep your child off-limits, and from "relaxing like Mommy and Daddy" when you're not looking, so make sure you don't forget to periodically check any mechanism that might pinch—or worse—curious little fingers.

As kids get older their playing or relaxing is more contained. Having easy-to-clean fabrics, stain-resistant carpet, and tables that can take abuse is still important. In the end, you will be more relaxed and they will be happier. ●

Measuring Up

Relaxing Dimension Guide

How much space do you really need to Right-Size and relax? Each drawing below shows various furniture layouts balancing your seating and the TV. Use at least the minimum (MIN) space needed for good placement of your sofa and chairs for comfort and usability.

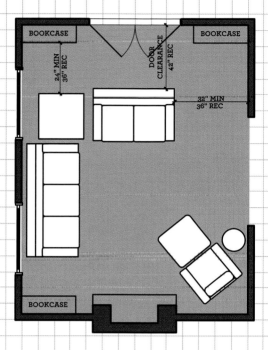

SOFA AND LOVESEAT

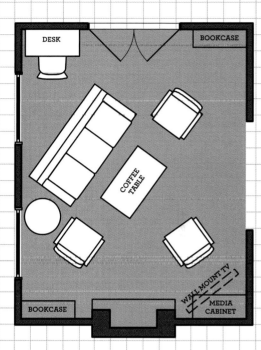

SOFA AND TWO CHAIRS

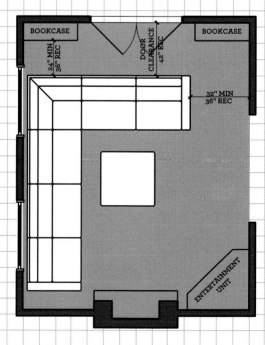

SECTIONAL

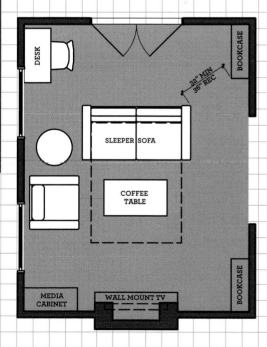

SLEEPER SOFA AND CHAIR

GENERAL TIPS:

- If the sofa feels too big for the room, try placing it on a diagonal
- Be sure to leave enough room to open a sleeper sofa
- Avoid a heavy or unwieldy coffee table in front of an often-used sleeper sofa
- If space is limited, use a console behind the sofa, instead of using end tables
- Comfortable, upholstered chairs that swivel are great for watching TV
- A storage ottoman is handy for bedding and pillows
- A wall-mounted TV saves surface space
- When fully open, wall hugging recliners take up less space
- Install dimmers on any overhead lighting; put three-way bulbs in lamps

HOME MADE

Make creative use of these modified stock cabinets, to design a craft room that covers all your needs. Cabinet inserts hold your supplies, large and small, and provide good workspace, too.

Consummate Crafter

Hands-On Activities

T ALL BEGAN SO INNOCENTLY. You barely felt it creeping upon you. Then one day you realized you couldn't keep your hands away from it. Soon you were swept up by the thrill of accomplishment, and waves of total enjoyment. And now, it has blossomed into an all-consuming passion! You are a proud and dedicated Consummate Crafter!

Whether your choice of relaxation is scrapbooking, decoupage, painting, beading, quilting, sewing, embroidery, weaving, or any of a hundred hobby choices, this is what excites you at the end of the day, or whenever you have some free time.

The problem is that your leisure activity is expanding fast. Supplies have grown from a few plastic boxes, to multitudes of them. Glue guns, tape, paper, articles, beads, threads, and boxes are piled up in different areas of your home. It's becoming difficult to stay on top of everything. Clearly, this passion needs a dedicated workspace of its own.

Do you have a separate space, a large closet, or a place you can close off from family and pet traffic?

MAKER'S MARK

Gift wrap requires rather careful handling, but if you store it away, it can be difficult and annoying to retrieve and use. If you can organize your papers and supplies, it will be much more fun to to wrap that gift.

STITCHING PRETTY

Keep order among your sewing supplies with this clever drawer insert allowing each color to have its own nesting place. It's much easier to keep track of what you need, and what you already have, with a system like this.

It would be ideal to have an entire room dedicated to your crafting, but most likely it is a shared space, such as a seldom-used guest room, a large laundry room, or even a quiet corner of the basement. Depending on the lighting you need, and the workspace required, the location might be as creative as the activity you pursue.

Ultimately, organization is key. Clutter happens with craft projects, especially when you cannot hope to complete the activity overnight, or even in a few days. Have you asked yourself where you are going to store all those craft supplies; where you can temporarily store your handiwork as you resume the rest of your life?

Dedicated shelving, built-in cabinets, or even a closet will help you contain your supplies. Clever cabinet inserts, originally designed for clothing, cosmetics, or jewelry, may be adapted for your specific needs. You might find a completely different, special interest activity with similar storage needs and suitable containers. For example, a friend who does beading found herself "borrowing" from her fly-fisherman husband's tackle boxes, for her smaller storage needs. The important thing is not to let it get out of hand, and to remain focused on containment.

It's also a good idea to plan a storage room with more space than you currently need, factoring in storage space for your finished projects, as well. This may sound a bit crazy, but before you know it, you will grow into it, and be perfectly at home with the fruits of your craft. ●

5

Couch Potato
Lounging Around

AR FROM BEING A FANTASY, YOU know the moments you spend as a Couch Potato are the transporting events of your existence, hurtling you into the euphoria that is beyond comfortable! You kick off your shoes, flop down on your favorite sofa, revel in the sheer bliss of stretching out, reach for that remote, and turn on the TV. Then a family member pops in to top off your beverage, or refill your bowl of chips and salsa. Ah, this is living!

Now that you've shed the cares of the day, let's think about that sofa. To get the best from it, make sure you can lay lengthwise without interference. Your height,

plus 12 inches, determines the minimum length needed for a good stretch. Let's not forget about the depth. The tallest member of the family will need the deepest sofa, so choose accordingly. Those who are height-challenged will need to be sitting against pillows, for proper comfort.

If your destination of calm is a big easy chair, how does it fit? How do your neck and back feel when you are settled in? Can you easily get into, and up from, the chair? Can you find a way to elevate your feet as well? Otherwise, a chair is just a chair. Add an ottoman or push back the recliner to that perfect "potato position," for mind and body.

SHOWY SEATING

A sectional can be a great way to enjoy the company of other Couch Potatoes, if you have room, and can sacrifice current seating alternatives.

Now, from your vantage point, take another look around you. Where is the nearest table? The coffee table should be within arm's reach, and large enough to handle at least one or two pizza boxes. The surface needs to be able to take real abuse from steaming-hot food and sweaty bottles, cans, or glasses without someone barking at you and disturbing your woolgathering. Likewise, the table near your chair or couch should verge on the indestructible, as it is likely to suffer the same abuse, along with enthusiastic pounding as you cheer on your team, or refuse to admit defeat. Storage beneath the table (or very close by) for plates, napkins, serving utensils, and the like makes good sense, too. Everyone knows that once you are in your spot, it's unlikely you'll ever leap up.

Lamps or overhead lighting should be managed much like the TV—by remote control, right from your chair. If the rigors of TV-watching prove too exhausting and you need to rest your eyes, turn it all off and catch up on your z's. Perhaps a nice blanket or throw, plucked from the storage ottoman that also serves as your foot rest, would make it all the more comfortable.

The next big challenge is making room for someone else. If it's a close friend, or your own small fry, then a sectional is just the answer. Before you zone out again, measure carefully and completely, to make sure this new seating plan fits into your space. Make sure the depth or width of the pieces can easily move through exterior and interior doors, without problems. If the sectional is going upstairs, take the stairwell into consideration, and any corners or curves that must be negotiated in the delivery process.

Of course, the danger of this expansion plan is that someone very close to you will claim equal time in his or her own chair, or spot on the couch.

You potatoes will have to sort that out! ●

FLEXIBLE FRIEND

It's not just about putting your feet up. You might also want the coziness of a throw. Hide it away in a nearby, handy storage ottoman, and no one will ever know how it disappeared.

GROUP ACTION

Share your space with a friend, but make sure your couch is large enough to accommodate both of you, with a "comfort zone" in-between.

Space Smarts

MAYBE YOU'VE NEVER EXPERIENCED THE surprise and disappointment of receiving a new piece of furniture, only to find it doesn't fit through the front door! But if you have, you never will forget it. You waited ages for that plush, inviting sofa or the softly padded recliner. Finally the piece showed up, but the deliverymen had nowhere else to put it, except in the garage, on the porch, or in the lobby. Blame it on love, or infatuation, because when you were in the furniture store, you surely weren't thinking clearly.

Somehow, when you saw it in the store, you totally forgot that the depth of the beautiful piece you had fallen in love with was 42 inches, and the front doorway has only a 36-inch clearance. No matter how the deliverymen twisted and turned, it just would not fit through that door. Maybe it fit through the patio doors (lucky, if you have them), but you still faced the predicament of negotiating the interior doors, which are generally only 30 inches wide, or less.

More dilemmas are posed by such impediments as hallways or stairs. Both upholstered pieces and case goods (tables, bureaus, armoires, storage pieces, and the like) are solidly constructed. The frames are joined with dowels or a combination of glue, staples, and/or corner blocks, which give it rigidity, not flexibility. It's quite difficult to turn a large piece of furniture around a sharp corner, or around staircase landings.

PERFECT FIT

This is what happens when you "eyeball" instead of accurately measuring the space you have for a new piece of furniture.

SPACED OUT

A Right-Sized sofa fits perfectly, even in a small room. Be sure to measure doorways and entrances, as well as the actual space it will occupy, before you buy the piece.

The third aspect of "fit-fullness" is the actual scale of the piece in your room. Someone told you that an oversized chair would add character and visual interest to a small room. What they forgot to mention, was that it would overpower the other, smaller-scaled furniture in the room. Perhaps you forgot the old, six-feet sofa fit the space perfectly, but you purchased one that measures seven feet. Now there's no room to move around it, let alone space for end tables. *What* were you thinking? (Note: furniture stores charge dearly for restocking—which may not even be an option!)

The answer to all these problems? Measure, measure, measure. *Before* you make a purchase, determine sizes of door openings, hall widths, turn space in corners, and the space you really have in your room for the new piece. Use your tape measure to make that paper bag model (see "How To Construct a Furniture Model," page 23) of the furniture you propose to buy; tell the salesperson you need to visualize it in your home, and have them give you exact measurements. As silly as it sounds, you will save yourself time, money, and anguish with this simple trick. You can immediately see whether it will fit through your patio doors or down the hall. Better yet, you can see if the piece—laid out on the floor in your family room—really fits or overwhelms.

Doing whatever it takes is worth avoiding an embarrassing phone call to the furniture store—and another interminable wait. ●

Now It's Your Turn

Right-Sizing *Your* Relaxing Area

RETHINKING THE DIFFERENT RELAXING AREAS AROUND YOUR house, means considering what works best for the way you live. Is the family room feeling cramped, because there just isn't room for everyone and their activities? Can your bedroom be rearranged to fit those two comfy chairs? Might that spare bedroom be the right spot for a great movie room, for just the two of you? Refer to the "Relaxing Style Audit," "Redesign Plan for Relaxing," and the "Relaxing Dimension Guide" in this chapter. You'll need to reinvent some unused or overused spaces to suit your own style, no matter how you relax. ●

Dedicated Area for Relaxing versus Multitasking Spaces

THINK DEDICATED CRAFTING CABINET

Containing this project-driven activity in a large, attractive cabinet, helps the part-time crafter keep projects organized and out of sight.

RESULT:
Allows more flexible space

RETHINK DEDICATED MEDIA CABINET

Moving a flat screen into the bedroom requires cabinets for storage of equipment and DVDs. The cabinet should blend with, but needn't match, existing furniture.

RESULT:
More space created

THINK MULTI-ACTIVITY CABINETS

A workroom by day, and a personal movie theater by night, calls for the clever use of cabinets to help keep both activities separate and contained.

RESULT:
More features in same space

Private Places

As home design has changed over the years, so has our sense of privacy. The bedroom and bathroom used to be completely closed off, the study was a space separate from family activities, and who wanted to visit your laundry room? Now the bathroom is for relaxation. The bedroom is a retreat. The home office is a requirement. The laundry has moved upstairs, and is readily available. Enjoy them all!

Where You Bathe

An interesting fact: *The bathroom has doubled in size over the last 30 years! Some of us have those supersized bathrooms, while some still have small ones. Sometimes, way too small. But it's not impossible to make it "right" for you, whatever the size.*

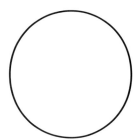

UR BATHROOMS, ONCE SO BASIC, HAVE grown not only in size but have become more glamorous, more indulgent. Let's blame the whirlpool tub for starting it all back in the 1980s. It fed our fantasies of candles, wine, and romance for more than two decades. We thought of our bath as a means of escape and relaxation.

The sad truth is our fast-paced, chock-full schedules do not allow time for a regular spa ritual. Besides, most of us today are trying to be more responsible in our use of water and energy. A giant whirlpool really doesn't make sense. It has become a bathing dinosaur. What many of us are looking for now are faster-filling, single-person soaking tubs or larger, fully-equipped showers as a smart replacement.

At the same time, many older homes still have a pint-sized main bathroom in its original five- by seven-feet size. Hard to believe, but this is less than the square footage of a king-sized mattress!

However incongruous, oversized master bathrooms continue to be a sign of prosperity in glossy magazines and on TV renovation programs. But they simply no longer fit today's lifestyles, and are (perhaps sadly) not used to full effect.

Clearly, many of our bathrooms need to be reevaluated, whether it's the cramped commode lacking the latest conveniences or the oversized, space-hogging spa. The mystery is how much is enough? How much is too much? That's what this chapter is all about. Take a moment to complete the "Bathing Style Audit" and "Bathroom Redesign Plan" on the following pages to determine your "type" or types of usage. This will guide you in considering changes that can turn your existing bathroom into one that really works for you and your family.

TESTING THE WATERS

Sleek, newer versions of the whirlpool combine an air bath with chromotherapy (mood-enhancing, projected, color light), for a luxury spa treatment at home, in half the space. Candles and fluffy towels are optional.

Bathing Style Audit

*Select the style that best reflects
your time spent in the bathroom. Then follow
the tips below for creating
more space and order, suited to that style.*

ARE YOU A BATHROOM MATE?

O Adapted to two different grooming styles
O Doesn't allow bath accessories to compete for space
O Need more towels available

TIPS:

- Plan on adequate work surface if using the bathroom together; allow 12 to 18 inches per person for "spread space"
- Consider a separate toilet area for privacy, if space permits; you will need at least 36 by 66 inches
- In the shower or tub, allow 18 inches additional shelf space for separate shampoos, conditioners, and soaps for both persons.
- Decant larger-bottled products into smaller containers for bathroom use; label and store together in the linen closet

ARE YOU A SPA SEEKER?

O Look for tranquility and peace
O The bathroom is the one place to shut out the world
O Need to unwind after a busy day

TIPS:

- Set aside 4 to 6 inches around the tub as adequate space for candles, bath salts or oils, and luxurious soaps
- If you use a mat for exercises, the workout space you need should be 2 feet longer than your height, and 2 feet wider than shoulder width
- Plan additional wall space (max. 39 by 20 by 5 inches) for a built-in towel warmer; 18 inches of storage area for a supply of massage towels
- For music, an iPod takes little counter space, but you'll need as much as 14 by 8 inches of wall space per speaker for a built-in system

ARE YOU A LENGTHY GROOMER?

O Prefer to use the bathroom for all grooming needs
O Need a place for everything
O Must have room for making up as well

TIPS:

- If you sit to apply makeup, lower part of work surface to 27 inches and tuck a bench beneath; if you stand, allow 18 inches for at-hand beauty supplies, and always store them in drawers
- Locate built-in waste basket in cabinetry for temporary garbage
- If wall space is available, install a recessed cabinet to hold the "smalls," allowing 35 to 40 inches for height, and 15 to 20 inches for width
- Think about adequate drawer space for small and large supplies; shallow drawers work for cosmetics; deeper ones hold larger bottles

ARE YOU AN EXPRESS BATHER?

O No lingering for you
O Make every second count
O Hate to lose time by rummaging around

TIPS:

- Have all grooming supplies at your fingertips, which means planning for a vanity with drawers rather than a pedestal sink; if you have a pedestal, consider a storage caddy on casters for supplies
- Upgrade your shower with an oversized showerhead and body sprays, for maximum effect in little time
- Make the most of space above the vanity with a mirrored cabinet that includes plug-ins for a hair dryer, shaver, toothbrush, and even a small LCD TV or radio.
- Don't forget to have a slip-resistant floor, for when you're in a hurry

ARE YOU A ROAD WARRIOR?

O Need multiples of travel size bath supplies
O Room for your toilet kit or kits
O Bathroom is another place to work

TIPS:

- Put travel supplies in a wire basket or labeled box under sink to make packing effortless; allow about 6 by 12 by 5 inches for each container
- Store medicines and vitamins for travel in compartmented dispensers in top drawer of vanity
- Store travel electronics near suitcases, not in bathroom
- Maintain two toilet kits: one for immediate short trips, and the other for lengthier ones; store the unused one with your other travel supplies; before heading home, place a note inside about replacement needs

Spa Seeker

The Tranquility Zone

OR A QUICK INTRODUCTION TO THE finer things in life, head to a luxurious spa. You'll never think about your bathroom in the same way again. Don't worry—the spa experience doesn't have to end so abruptly. You can take home some of the sumptuousness of a spa, and that's not to suggest you steal the towels!

For the Spa Seeker, the main ingredient is a new deluxe whirlpool tub with an aromatherapy system, and an air bath feature. This means you need a lot of room for this type of rest and relaxation. A freestanding, deep, soaker tub needs space around it, and special plumbing,

but don't let that deter you. If space is tight, opt for a deeper, built-in tub, which provides the same stress reduction in a smaller space.

Promise yourself to try out the tub before you buy it. Shed your inhibitions in the showroom, and step into your favorite model. Does it feel comfortable? Is your back resting at the right angle? Is your neck or head supported when you recline? You can't tell this by simply looking.

If you have an even smaller space, think of a vertical spa experience by customizing your shower. A combination of multifunction showerheads, body sprays, and a sophisticated temperature control system will provide you with relaxation in a spa-like haven.

WATER SIGNS

Perfect for a good long soak, this spotlight-grabbing tub promises spa indulgence. Add instant glamour to your bathroom with a mixture of matte and gloss tile, and stone, in creamy tranquil hues.

INNER PEACE

Luxurious details and dramatic scale give this vanity a real presence. The hefty marble top supports two glass vessel sinks, which shimmer in the downlighting. Two elegant faucets complement the sink height. Choose a light-colored vanity to visually expand this space.

WARM UP

Enjoy the luxury of toasty towels with this electric warming drawer. It's an easy enhancement to any spa bathroom.

Bath time should be a precious time—a moment to escape from the outside world. You can personalize your relaxation with other elements of an actual spa getaway. Attention to details of the vanity, and subtle storage, are more important than the specialty-scented potions and lotions you have gathered. Those come later.

Maximize the spa potential with closed and open storage. Hidden away is all the clutter that you may have accumulated. Remember—you never spot a litter of bottles in a spa. And out in the open are plush cotton towels, which envelop you in comfort.

Consider the height of the vanity as well. Bending down to wash or brush your teeth detracts from the ease and comfort you desire.

Surfaces should be smooth—not rough—in a spa bath, and floor and countertop surfaces need to complement the cabinetry in color and texture. Matte or polished stone is favored in upscale spas. To get that same look, use eggshell finish paint, or try the new, subtle colors of

high-definition laminate as less-expensive substitutes. Regardless, keep the majority of surfaces light, to create a soothing atmosphere of bare essentials.

Lighting can make a dramatic change to the look and feel of your spa bathroom. Install dimmers then set a soft and diffused level for creating a sensual mood, or brighten for shaving or applying makeup.

Warmth is one of the unmentioned elements of spa design, and is something that you can easily incorporate into your own bath. In Europe, towel warmers are a popular way to heat a bathroom as a substitute for a radiator. You may not want to eliminate existing heating, but a towel warmer operates on pennies a day, and to great effect. Electric towel warming drawers are now on the market, and do the same thing in a more concentrated space.

Floors gently warmed by radiant heating are equally sybaritic, but require a full remodel. If you are doing so, the results are more than worth the investment, even in the smallest of bathrooms.

As a last touch, create the atmosphere of a spa with scented soaps and candles. Be sure to keep your chosen scents in the same family of fragrance so they don't clash with one another. There is nothing worse than feeling like you are being overwhelmed in a flower shop, rather than lulled into a reverie. ●

Bathroom Redesign Plan

Before you start planning to change your bathroom, look at the lists below. The items you check should help guide you in assessing your space, and how it might work best for you. Use these responses to define the problems, as well as the solutions.

Reasons for making a change?
(check all that apply)
- Entire bathroom is too small
- Arrangement is not functional
- Lack of storage and counter space
- Fixtures are outdated or unappealing
- Plumbing problems
- Bathroom tile is worn and dated
- Insufficient hot water supply
- Inadequate lighting or electrical outlets
- Add or remove a fixture

Who uses this room?
(check all that apply)
- Adults
- Older adults
- Children
- Guests
- Pets

How is it used?
(check all that apply)
- Bathing children
- Bathing older adults
- Showering
- Both bathing and showering
- Grooming
- Makeup
- Relaxing in whirlpool, steam, or sauna
- Cat litter or water bowl

What do you need to store here?
(check all that apply)
- Toiletries
- Medicines/vitamins
- First aid items
- Cleaning supplies
- Paper supplies
- Towels
- Bed linens
- Grooming accessories

What do you need for more comfort?
(check all that apply)
- Better lighting
- Good ventilation
- More counter space
- More storage space
- More floor space
- Separate vanity, if shared
- Adult-height vanity
- Adequate mirrors
- Slip-resistant flooring
- Easy-access shower
- Larger shower
- Air bath or whirlpool
- Safe-exit bathtub
- Soaking tub
- More towel bars
- Well-placed grab bars
- More privacy

Trade-Offs

As you map out a plan for Right-Sizing your bathroom, think about the trade-offs below. Remember to take into consideration the amount of space you really have, while weighing wants versus needs.

VERSUS		VERSUS	
Sink In Vanity ⟷ **Pedestal Sink**		**Whirlpool Tub** ⟷ **Bathtub**	
More storage space	Sleeker design	Deeper and more relaxing	Less expensive
Vessel Sink ⟷ **Undermount Sink**		**Whirlpool Tub** ⟷ **Air Bath**	
Added height	More work surface	Noisier and larger bubbles	Quieter, smaller bubbles
Lever-Handled Faucet ⟷ **Knob-Handled Faucet**		**Tub-Shower** ⟷ **Freestanding Shower**	
Easier to grasp	Takes less space	Restricted shower space	Larger shower space
Rounded-Front Toilet ⟷ **Elongated Toilet**		**Wall-Mounted Showerhead** ⟷ **Hand-Held Showerhead**	
Space saver	More convenient for men	Limited range of spray	Adjustable for height
Toilet In Bathroom ⟷ **Separate Toilet Room**		**Ceiling-Mounted Showerhead** ⟷ **Wall-Mounted Showerhead**	
Space maker	More privacy	One-directional spray	Multidirectional spray

6

SMART SPACE

Groom at the clean, European-style, wall-hung double sinks with storage beneath. Convenient shelves and right-height mirror make it easy. The nearby toilet keeps all close at hand.

Express Bather

Easy In, Easy Out

WHO HAS TIME these days? Certainly not you! From the moment your feet hit the ground, you're moving fast—really fast. That's certainly true in your first stop of the day—your own bathroom! Everything needs to be planned for efficiency and speed.

As an Express Bather, you don't want to linger and have to search for everyday items. The radio is already on, bringing you news and traffic updates as you brush your teeth. Because multitasking is your nature, look for cabinetry that allows you to have everything in order. The mirror or mirrored bath cabinet should be placed at the "right," comfortable height as well, with no clutter on the countertop to slow you down.

MIRROR IMAGE

This double bath cabinet has it all. It lifts up from the bottom for easy access. The bottom shelf includes electrical outlets for plug-and-play. Handy pendant lights don't add glare in the mirror.

The shower also needs to function well with thermostatic controls for the proper water temperature. Think about a showerhead that gives you precisely the quick, easy spray you want, to get you on your way. Multiple towels sit in readiness and easy access as you turn off the water. Ten minutes down...

Maybe you don't consider the toilet as a time-saver, but the latest generation of water-saving toilets have new features to do just that. The soft-close toilet seat automatically lowers to be ready for the next occupant. Dual-flush toilets offer two levels of water flushing as needed. Consider a wall-hung toilet for your comfort height if placed in a larger bathroom.

Lighting controls that turn off automatically after a period of time are a good buy for the Express Bather, as is an electronic exhaust system. You don't have to worry about whether you left that light or fan on, as you zoom ahead to dress for the day.

If you are the kind of person who needs a full blast of information as you shave or wash, then having all those electronics close at hand is the answer. New bath cabinets have electrical outlets already installed, and all you have to do is preprogram your favorite channels or stations. Other electronics, such as hair dryers, toothbrushes, or razors can sit on a shelf in a charged position awaiting your arrival. If you store them elsewhere, keep them all together and plan for enough Ground Fault Interrupt (GFI) outlets for speedy grooming.

If your bathroom has pedestal sinks instead of a vanity, you need to think about creative use of small storage units that expand your at-hand supplies, when at the sink for that final touch-up. Extra washcloths, soap, and sundries can be near, but not in your way. Put your watch back on and check your timing. Twenty minutes in and out, but then who was counting? ●

HOT SEAT

Keep the toilet area clutter-free with a closed wastebasket, and toilet paper at arms reach. Select a comfort-height commode for easy on and off.

Bathroom Mate
Dual Outlook

NO MAJOR WARS HAVE been fought over who gets dibs on the bathroom, but many battles *have* been fought. Given the choice, does anyone really want to share a bathroom? Like it or not, the reality is a shared bathroom brings people together in a most personal way—Mom and Dad, two siblings, or even parents and children.

The ideal solution for children is to have two separate sinks, and a common shower and toilet space. Home builders call this a "Jack and Jill" bathroom, typical in many new homes. For the parents, with conflicting schedules and different expectations as to who gets to use what and when, it comes down to big-time compromise. For some lucky couples, harmony is predicated on totally separate bathrooms, a real luxury of space.

If Bathroom Mates can agree on a marriage of styles, the rest of the decisions will be somewhat easier. You have lots of beauty supplies, you get more storage space; he likes to use lots of towels, so the hamper is on his side. Arguments about who gets more counter or storage space can be avoided by sticking to the agreed upon

DOUBLE TAKE

This kids' bath promotes real cooperation, with ample space for both. The lower showerhead works for younger users.

SERIOUS FUN

The handrail on this recessed tub, designed as a mini swimming pool, acts as a grab bar.

EQUAL SHARES

This master bath is designed as "separate but equal." Each person gets his or her own area. The real compromise is that shower and tub areas are minimum size, and sink space is communal.

"division of real estate." We're not even dealing with the toilet-seat-up-or-down issue—that's a battle that may never be won!

Privacy issues about toilet use can be a source of conflict, so many couples decide on a separate toilet room. Can you share a single sink, or do you each need your own? How about the counter space between the sinks? This neutral territory is the ideal spot for common items.

You bathe and he showers. This can be a problem when you're on the same schedule. If you are remodeling, choose a smaller tub and pedestal sink to make room for a separate shower. No matter the space, using it wisely can become a perfect partnership. ●

UNITED FRONT

Because this couple doesn't use the bathroom at the same time, the answer here was to share the sink space, but divide up the storage drawers equally between them.

Kid Smarts

JUST LIKE GROWN-UPS, KIDS need a bathroom that really works for them. It should be functional and safe first, decorative second.

Start with a non-skid floor and mat in this wet world. Tub mats keep little feet from slipping in the bath, as do adhesive pads that stick to the tub bottom, with grab bars for holding on. Faucet covers are important as well, to keep kids from accidentally turning on the hot water. Electrical outlets need attention, and covering for toddlers. Consider a built-in nightlight and ventilation, and lights on timers, too.

Don't even be tempted to decorate tiles to taps with the latest kiddies' theme. If you do go overboard,

SMALL WONDERS

If you can't resist buying a tiny toilet, plan ahead with plumbing choices, allowing you to convert to a standard-sized toilet in a few years.

KIDDING AROUND

The better choice for a kid's bath is an undermount sink in a cabinet, so they can effortlessly reach the sink with or without a stool. Add a single-handle faucet, because it is easier for children to handle than one with separate hot and cold controls—with or without a frog!

remember that children grow up fast, and their tastes change even faster—and you will *have* to renovate! Be practical, investing in character-driven shower curtains, or thematic towels and toothbrushes instead.

Select standard-sized fixtures so you don't have to replace them in a few years. Think about a one-piece, elongated-bowl toilet that sits lower to the floor. They are better for toilet-training. When installing a toilet, keep more than 30 inches between the wall and cabinet. Leaving 42 inches allows an adult enough space to assist a tot with early toilet duties. The good news is this commode will still be comfortable for other kids and adults.

We start out bathing children in a tub, and they graduate to showers when no longer needing our help. Think ahead by installing an adjustable showerhead, or more than one showerhead. This means the shower can grow with the child. If space is an issue, a tub/shower combination is a better choice, rather than having one of each.

Kids need storage too. Over-the-door hangers and wall-mounted peg hooks are helpful for towels and robes. And all the tub toys? Keep them accessible in a plastic bin under the sink, or in a hanging mesh bag. Later, storage needs will shift to include more personal care items such as shampoos, conditioners, soaps, and body washes—and before you know it—hair dryers, shavers, and much more. ●

Lengthy Groomer

Bathed in Beauty

VISUALIZE THE extravagance of having time to pamper yourself on a regular basis. Most of us can only dream of this luxury. The truth is that you have a very busy life, with too many demands on your schedule, whether at home or in the outside world. Despite your best efforts, you don't have the leisure to schedule a spa treatment, or even a pedicure, so your bathroom becomes the site for all of your necessary beauty treatments. You remember your own mother having "beauty nights," and you understand now—only too well—how wonderfully therapeutic they can be.

If you are, or aspire to be, a Lengthy Groomer, having the space to give yourself a manicure or pedicure is an absolute necessity, not an indulgence. On a temporary basis, block out the world. Turn off your cell phone, computer, and any other distraction. Start by treating yourself to a soaking foot bath. Put those full-body sprays on "high" in your spacious shower, and let the water massage away the cares of the day. You're feeling better already.

Turn the lights down low and listen to soft music. All those tensions slide down the drain. Now slip into a plush, velvety-soft robe. Sound dreamy? If so, you really need some spoiling—and if you don't do it, who will?

GO WITH THE FLOW

This oversized shower replaced an unused whirlpool tub. Its multiple shower heads give a variety of bathing experiences. The heavy-duty glass doors roll with ease on imported metal casters, and the glass enclosure makes the room seem even larger. The teak floor is slip-resistant, and the companion fold-up seat adds a convenient place to shave. The foot bath, adjacent to the shower, is relaxing all by itself.

Do you have everything you will need at your fingertips? Not just your favorite scented lotions, perfumed shower gels, or fragrant soaps, but your manicure and pedicure tools should be close at hand in your vanity.

It's time to turn up those lights a bit, and get busy. A generous, magnifying mirror turns the practice of reviewing any slight imperfection into a clear, simple action. Wouldn't a small bench on which to rest your toes be helpful? Of course, extra, super-plush spa towels are essential.

Perhaps tonight is the night to dip your hands into a hot wax bath, then rest nearby savoring the warmth of the wax on your mitted, deliciously-soft hands. Close your eyes for a minute or two and let the moment soothe you.

DISPLAY CASE

Think about the storage area for towels and sundries. If your home doesn't include a linen closet, consider recycling an unused armoire, now that it no longer holds the TV, into a decorative linen space.

Before you head back into the real world, enjoy the peace and quiet of your bathing environment. There should be nothing harsh here to disrupt your reverie. The softly tinted tile, pale-veined stone, or creamy-colored cabinetry help you create that soothing setting. Your exhaust system—on a timer—allows you to have the right level of humidity without worrying about turning it off. The controlled lighting creates a dynamic, visual environment.

Perhaps the final extravagance is the radiant heat system in the floors. No more chilly floor for your now-perfect toes. Your bare feet appreciate the warm surface! And you may not want to admit it right now, but your favorite pet has discovered the magic of these floors as well. Are you ready to open the door and let in the world? ●

OPEN WIDE

These salon-type, pullout cabinets help you store all the essentials for your pampering sessions, with style. This expands your space and frees your countertop from clutter.

Measuring Up
Bathroom Dimension Guide

How much space do you really need to Right-Size your bathroom? The drawings below show typical layouts, with minimum (MIN) and recommended (REC) values for comfort and usability. This information is for planning purposes only. Be sure to check local or state building codes.

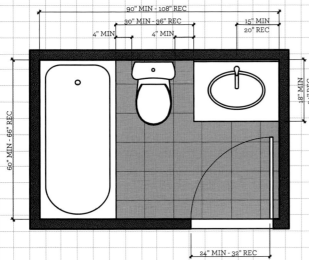

SMALL BATHROOM

- Consider reversing entry door swing to increase room
- Use area behind door for hidden storage
- Hooks require less space than towel bars

TOILET ROOM

- Use space above toilet for supply storage
- The room takes more space than a freestanding toilet
- Remember to add more light and an exhaust system

POWDER ROOM

- Plan for a shelf or some surface for purses
- Adequate mirror will help expand the space
- Dark-colored walls make the room seem smaller

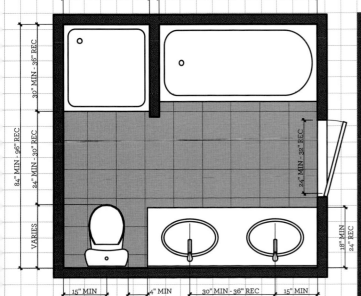

MEDIUM-SIZED BATHROOM

- Have only one sink in a double vanity for more counter space
- Combine tub and shower for more room
- Separate toilet from vanity with knee wall for privacy

GENERAL TIPS:

- For more space inside, swing the door out
- Hooks or pegs take up less space than bars, for hanging towels
- Leave more room between fixtures for ease of bathing, and toilet-training tots
- A dimmer or permanent night light makes middle-of-the-night visits less jarring
- Use wall space above the toilet for a storage cabinet or shelf unit
- Remember a shelf or small table in the powder room
- Install twin medicine cabinets over twin sinks, for more amicable mornings

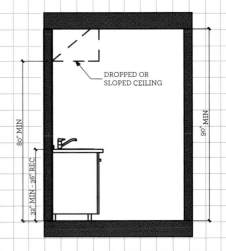

CLEARANCE FOR VANITY

- Allow enough space for headroom above vanity
- Storage above vanity should be within easy reach
- Lighting in this area should not create shadows

Road Warrior

On The Road Again

AS GLAMOROUS AS IT MAY sound, being on the road for endless days is not really wonderful at all. You long for your own space, especially when it comes to the bathroom. Yes, the hotels may offer enticing amenities, but there is no place like home, with your own gear and gadgets, even if it's only for a few days. Then, of course, it is up and out again.

If you are a Road Warrior, having a quiet environment from which to move forth is key. When you have to get up in what seems like the middle of the night, you need everything to be close at hand, with replacement supplies already packed. No scrambling at 4 AM!

Did you remember your vitamins or medicines? How about some hand sanitizer? Luckily, you've created a small drawer for everything you need when you travel, and each supply has its own place. This is no time to look for missing items. In fact, you tucked a checklist in that drawer as a reminder you can quickly scan, to be sure you'll have everything you need.

In order to maintain peace and quiet during your morning ablutions, lest you wake someone in the adjacent bedroom, a quieter-flushing toilet is a prerequisite. New dual-flush versions operate with a hushed sound. When you use the bathroom exhaust for your shower, having one with variable power allows for less noise. Even your home electronics are selected for their lower noise levels. Keep them handy in your bath cabinet, already plugged in. Although you can probably dress with your eyes shut, you do need adequate light in the bathroom. Install a dimmer for softer illumination in those early morning hours.

Now imagine waking up to the smell of fresh-brewed coffee! One amenity you have installed is a little breakfast bar. It was formerly an alcove used for storage. Using the same style cabinetry, it is nicely integrated into the bathroom decor. Flip that switch on the brewer and reach

IN CONTROL

Imagine plugging your electronics directly into an outlet in your bath cabinet, for total ease and convenience.

BASIN INSTINCT

Even in low light set by a dimmer, it's easy to access necessary toiletries and supplies from this adult-height vanity. Extra built-in cabinets are cleverly recessed into the wall on the left.

for a bit of juice from the fridge below, before you hop into the shower. It saves you precious time and avoids you making a trip to the kitchen. Ready? Then it's off you go!

One of the benefits of being a Road Warrior is that you are exposed to a variety of bathroom designs. Hotels pack a lot of function into fairly small spaces. If you've paid attention to the layouts of your favorite on-the-road baths, you know that a motion-sensor bath exhaust is one of those hidden amenities you can bring to your own bathroom.

You might like having a rack for extra towels in the shower, instead of rummaging in a closet. How about eye-level baskets in the shower for your shampoo and conditioner, which holds them at a convenient height? Certainly, keeping the counter space at an adult height of 36 inches, rather than the 27 inches like many bathroom vanities, is better for your back. Extra electrical outlets make sense as well, when protected by GFI. You are on your own when it comes to scented soaps, lotions, and loofahs. ●

COFFEE MATE

Imagine the real convenience of your own mini kitchen (or breakfast bar) with a sink, small fridge, microwave, and coffee maker close at hand; think about locating it adjacent to the bathroom for that quick cup of coffee in the morning. Why go all the way to the kitchen for that Sunday morning Mimosa?

Guest Smarts

IF YOU WANT TO REALLY ASSESS how you treat your guests, visit your own guest bathroom. Is it filled with unnecessary "stuff"—a bowl of aging potpourri (so yesterday), a plastic flower arrangement (probably dusty), petrified toothpaste, very tired towels, a crocheted toilet paper cover? If you borrowed your style from a bed and breakfast visit years ago, it's time to rethink and refresh.

How about the home's smallest space, the powder room? Usually this pint-sized space is an over-decorated showplace, with dried-up shards of soap or over-starched hand towels, intimidating visitors into using toilet paper to wipe their hands!

You need to actually use these rooms as though you were your own guest. Walk into that powder room with your handbag to repair your makeup, as a visitor might. Hard to see in the dim light? Where did you put that purse down? If the toilet paper ran out, was there a spare?

When you check out the guest bath, bring the toilet kit and grooming essentials you would pack if you were actually visiting. Take a shower, brush your teeth, and apply makeup. You may experience a shock. All these years, your long-suffering guests never said a word—a clean change of clothes in a pile on the floor, the hair dryer balanced on the back of the sink, the towel out of reach on the opposite wall.

PILING ON THE PERKS

Guests need, at the least, fresh towels, but also a place to put them when they are dirty. A hamper comes in handy for guests as well as for ourselves, and make room for a little basket of toiletries guests may have forgotten.

For inspiration, consider hotels you remember fondly. A sink installed off-center allows more usable counter space. A mirror-lined wall, with touch-latch cabinets provides room for extra supplies, creating an illusion of spaciousness. A little basket of fresh toiletries pampers guests, and furnishes what they may have forgotten.

The average powder room measures about 20 square feet, but there are only two fixtures to fit in it: a toilet and a sink. Take a look at how the door swings. How easy or difficult is it to maneuver around the door as you step through? If it's a tight squeeze, you might consider swinging the door out, or changing it for a pocket door that slides into the wall.

Clearly, space is at a premium. How about a wall-hung sink or a pedestal lavatory, instead of a sink in a vanity cabinet? Necessities like hand towels, toilet paper, soap, etc. need a place to hide. A shallow storage cabinet, recessed between the joists, takes up little or no room. If you have a little more space, a small cart on wheels adds a smart touch for storing supplies.

It may be the small upgrades that achieve the desired effect in your powder room or guest bath, rather than an expensive and dramatic overhaul. At the end of the day, what we all want is for these rooms to be a great way to welcome guests without saying a word. ●

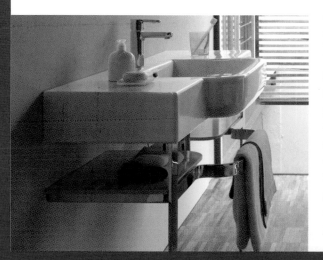

TAKE A POWDER

When space is at a premium, think about a wall-hung or a pedestal sink, instead of one in a vanity cabinet. Remember—necessities like hand towels, toilet paper, soap, paper cups, etc. need a place to hide.

Now It's Your Turn

Right-Sizing *Your* Bathroom

NOW IT'S TIME TO FOCUS ON YOUR BATHROOM, OR bathrooms. No matter the size of your spaces, there never seems to be enough room for all your needs and wants. Smaller baths pose their own interesting design challenges, while larger ones present equally demanding opportunties to function better. If you have already completed the "Bathing Style Audit" and "Bathroom Redesign Plan," your needs versus your wants should be clearer. Let's look at how to achieve that bathroom of your dreams within the space you have. ●

1. Bathing versus Showering

THINK DEDICATED SHOWER

In a smaller bath, there is usually a tub and shower combination in one space. To create a (possibly) more satisfying shower experience, you might elect to get rid of the tub itself. Make the shower the center of attention. Don't keep the tub for resale value only. Think of this as a vertical spa.

RESULT:
No extra space needed

RETHINK SHOWER/TUB COMBO

Some of the latest generation of higher-end tubs have a showering component, which is separate, but used in the same space. If you are considering replacing an unused double whirlpool tub, this might be an answer. You would then have a single massage tub, plus a separate shower.

RESULT:
More function in same space

THINK DEDICATED TUB

The new stand-alone or built-in soaking tubs come in a variety of sizes. If your preferred mode is to bathe only, this is a good choice. You will need less space if your tub is built-in. A freestanding one requires more breathing space around it, plus floor space for the tub filler.

RESULT:
Need a little more space

2. Single versus Double Sink Vanities

THINK ONE SINK ONLY

This may be your only choice in a small bath, but if you have room, consider extra countertop space instead of adding another sink. Most of us rarely use both at the same time, except in a shared or children's bath.

RESULT:
More space to maneuver

RETHINK DOUBLE SINK COMBO

Where space is not so tight, rather than selecting companion sinks in a countertop, separate the sinks into two cabinets with built-in storage in between. This gives each person their individual area, without competition.

RESULT:
Uses slightly more space

3. Toilet Placement

THINK GLASS WALL

Even in the smallest bathroom, there is usually room for a ½ inch-thick, laminated or frosted glass wall, dividing the toilet from the sink area. While not creating genuine privacy, it crafts the illusion of separate spaces.

RESULT:
No extra space needed

THINK TOILET ROOM

This is not an option for a smaller bathroom, unless you would be willing to give up a large, nearby linen closet. In a larger bath, include separate venting for white noise and odor control.

RESULT:
More space needed

4. More Storage

THINK BEHIND-THE-DOOR

The area behind the entry door in any bath is untapped space. A tall, narrow cabinet, recessed between studs, provides room for smaller-sized supplies. The door can be outfitted with shallow, wire shelving for bulky items.

RESULT:
More space added

RETHINK CABINETRY BENEATH SINK

New cabinet inserts maximize existing space with better organization of drawer and door areas, giving you easy access to frequently used items in the sink area.

RESULT:
No extra space needed

THINK MIRROR STORAGE

Mirrors appear to expand space. A large mirrored area above the sink can do double-duty, if you install storage cabinets with touch-latch openers behind it.

RESULT:
More function in same space

Where You Sleep

Gone is the bedroom just reserved for sleeping! *In its place is a multifunctional haven that works, plays, exercises, relaxes, or whatever. Whether your bedroom is too small or too big, use Right-Sizing ideas to make it "right" for you.*

W HEN IT COMES TO SLEEPING, let's face it: we do it all over the house. Well, maybe not in the laundry room or kitchen, but most other spaces are deemed suitable for a short nap or even longer sleep. Who of us would not admit to snoozing on their super-cushy sofa, or dozing on their comfy recliner, wherever they may be located? After soaking in a long bath, wouldn't it be nice to rest on a terry-covered chaise in that big bathroom? I have even caught a few winks myself, after a stupendous holiday meal, right at the dining table while pretending to listen to dinner companions. When caught, I complained the chair was just too comfortable.

With all that competition, where does that leave the bedroom? It's no longer just a room for sleeping. Many of us use it as a relaxing space after work to collapse—reading the mail or magazines, eating supper, and of course watching TV. The dog or cat knows best because they are already there, testing the pillow-top comfort.

The master bedroom has grown in size in order to accommodate the dramatic, architectural headboard and bed. There was a time that bed even fought for space with the big, bad armoire—home of the giant TV—but that fight has been resolved. The armoire withdrew in favor of a sleek flat screen TV. Still, some masters sport fireplaces and a couple of companion chaises.

Change is on the way again in the master bedroom. The bed still occupies one-third of the space, but where have the traditional dresser and chest of drawers gone? They have been given up in favor of a dressing room (or two) with built-ins. Instead of scrambling from drawer to drawer, everything is almost in one place... until the next big transformation.

Start now with the "Style Audit" and "Redesign Plan" on the following pages, to find out your "type" or types of usage. This will guide you in considering changes that can turn your bedrooms into ones that really work for you.

NEAT DREAMS

You don't have to be a princess to enjoy this stunning poster bed. It's well-dressed in fine, white linens, and provides all the comforts of home. Television watching or reading are optional.

Sleeping Style Audit

Select the sleeping style that best reflects you. Then follow the tips below for creating more space and order, suited for that style.

ARE YOU A BEDROOM MATE?

O Adapts to two different sleeping styles
O Needs compromise on mattress firmness
O Separate, but not-so-equal, storage space

TIPS:

- Consider the height of the taller person and add 3 or 4 inches to determine the length of the bed, and therefore, mattress size
- To make best use of available closet space or furniture, allow 50% for double hanging space, 25% for single hanging space, and 25% for shelf storage
- Find a bed that is stable and solid in construction, with headboard bolted securely to the rails; check additional measurements to make sure all pieces of the bed can fit through halls, doors, and up stairs; if your partner snores, try ear plugs or invest in a sound machine to create a more peaceful environment

ARE YOU A SLEEPING BEAUTY?

O Want a place to shut out the world
O Bedroom should be a room of beauty
O Need to unwind at the end of a busy day

TIPS:

- Plan on a full-length mirror on back of bedroom door, or within closet if possible
- Divide clothes storage so informal lounging gear is readily available; keep robes on hooks or hangers for easy access, but not hidden away
- Create space for an end-of-bed bench to keep quilt or duvet, as well as temporary storage of decorative pillows
- Use a headboard that is comfortable, as well as supportive

ARE YOU A ROAD WARRIOR?

O Need suitcase and travel wardrobe, plus supplies, in easy access
O Require room to spread out in preparation for packing
O Want a comfortably dark bedroom as soundproof as possible

TIPS:

- Have a stable bench or tabletop in or near the closet to support your suitcase; make sure dimensions accommodate the largest bag
- Organize closet so travelling clothes are separated, and available as needed; keep a list of clothes at cleaners/laundry to avoid surprises
- Create better closet lighting for late-night arrivals or early-morning departures
- Be sure to have a reliable alarm or clock radio with easy-to-read dials on your bedside table; allow 18 to 24 inches of width for electronics

ARE YOU A NIGHT OWL?

O Like to read in bed or watch TV late at night
O Interrupted sleep patterns
O Frequently need quiet "thinking time"

TIPS:

- Place lighting on dimmers or use motion sensors to see when arising in the middle of the night—preventing trips or falls
- Have wireless headphones and remote control in easy access with a notepad and pen or pencil at your bedside; bedside table should be at least 32 inches high for comfortable reach
- Plan on non-bed, alternative seating for reading or watching TV; make sure you have a comfortable chair, and perhaps an ottoman, plus adequate lighting
- If you need to have a laptop at your fingertips, reserve space for outlets and rechargers near or on the bedside table

ARE YOU A SECRET NAPPER?

O Find short amounts of sleep very refreshing
O Do not necessarily require a bed to sleep well
O Must have a neck roll and throw for comfort

TIPS:

- Install carpet and adequate draperies to deaden sound and insulate the room for better sleep; turn off ringer on landline phone, and silence your cell phone
- Make sure you have adequate ventilation in the room; think about including a ceiling fan for better air circulation
- Consider blackout shades for daytime sleeping
- Your favorite napping spot should be the right size for comfort, whether stretching out or curling up on a chaise or couch; take your measurements, allowing about 6 to 8 inches more than your height, for a comfortable stretch

Sleeping Beauty
Bedroom Bliss

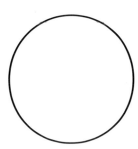

NE OF THE GREAT lessons I learned from fairy tales was that the heroine always got a good night's sleep. No matter what danger she was in or what was in store for her the next day, she simply slept well. No visions of bills to be paid, laundry to be done, or an overscheduled upcoming day! If you have aspirations of recapturing the Sleeping Beauty in you without that evil spell, then pay attention.

The bedroom has become more than a place for a good night's rest. It is a safe haven from the fast pace of your various lives. It's a place to soothe your soul. If you are a Sleeping Beauty, you recognize the need for a perfect escape—an uncluttered and simple space that does not intrude on your enjoyment of the room.

Start off with a great bed. It is the focal point of your bedroom, and probably the most important furniture purchase you will make. If it is true that you spend one-third of your life in bed sleeping, then why not make it an extraordinary experience. Your bed deserves to have the "wow" factor.

Choose a style that fits your personality—be it romantic with a canopy, or rustic with painted wood, elegant carving, or sleek metal. Before you fall in love

BEAUTY SLEEP

Climb onto a luxurious bed with a spectacular mattress, and you will feel regal. Make sure that your headboard is supportive, as well as soft, for a quick read before dreaming.

DRESS TO IMPRESS

Use a corner of your dressing room as an evening clothes closet. The drawers below hold all your accessories: bags, belts, and jewels.

with your bed, check on the need for a box spring for support—not all beds need one. Mattresses have grown more sumptuous lately, measuring from 8 to a fat 19 inches thick. The mattress alone may work in a contemporary bed frame.

Select remaining furniture to enhance the main attraction—your bed. Position your bedside tables or small chests symmetrically on either side of the bed for a sense of balance. Storage furniture should visually recede, and be a stain or color complementary to the bed itself. The latest trend is to minimize the once-required double or triple dresser and chest of drawers. Built-in storage is a terrific option if your closet size and layout permit. This leaves the bedroom area with a freer, more open look.

The flat screen TV helped drive to extinction the once-necessary armoire, commonly used to house bulkier televisions. Recycle that big piece of furniture into a linen closet, or out-of-season clothing storage, but get it out of the bedroom, please. You will need wall space to hang your flat screen or another piece of scaled-down furniture, slightly wider than the new TV, on which to rest it.

Now, lie back and relax. ●

MIRROR MIRROR

Even a storybook princess needs to see herself from hairdo to shoes. A mirror in your closet helps you make quick and easy touch-ups.

Bedroom Redesign Plan

Before you start planning to change your bedroom, look at the lists below. The items you check should help guide you in assessing your space, and how it might work best for you. Use these responses to define the problems, as well as the solutions.

Reasons for making a change?

(check all that apply)

○ Bedroom is too small
○ Bedroom is too large
○ Arrangement is not functional
○ Lack of storage for clothes
○ Fixtures are outdated or unappealing
○ Privacy problems
○ Bedroom is not dark enough
○ Flooring is worn or dated
○ Inadequate lighting/electrical outlets
○ Television is out of date

Who uses this room?

(check all that apply)

○ Adults
○ Older adults
○ Children
○ Guests
○ Pets

How is it used?

(check all that apply)

○ Sleeping
○ Napping
○ Reading
○ Working
○ Watching TV
○ Exercising
○ Eating
○ Make-up/grooming

What do you need to store here?

(check all that apply)

○ Everyday clothes
○ Evening clothes
○ Underwear/hosiery
○ Bulky sweaters
○ Shoes
○ Belts/ties
○ Jewelry
○ Out-of-season clothes

What do you need for more comfort?

(check all that apply)

○ Better mattress
○ More storage space
○ Adequate or improved lighting
○ Carpeting
○ Reading chair
○ Flat screen TV
○ Innovative bedside tables
○ Fresh window coverings
○ Less furniture
○ Chaise for napping or lounging
○ Built-in storage
○ Better light control
○ Fireplace
○ Telephone/computer access

Trade-Offs

As you map out a plan for Right-Sizing your bedroom, think about the trade-offs below. Remember to take into consideration the amount of space you really have, while weighing wants versus needs.

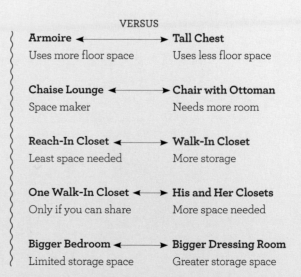

VERSUS

Queen-Sized Bed ◄───► **King-Sized Bed**
More bedroom space | More sleeping space

Twin Beds ◄───► **Double or Full-Sized Bed**
Less bedroom space | More bedroom space

Sleeper Sofa ◄───► **Pull-Down Murphy Bed**
Extra seating | Loss of wall space

Bedside Tables ◄───► **Bedside Chests**
Space saver | More storage

Triple Dresser ◄───► **Built-In Storage**
Less bedroom space | More bedroom space

VERSUS

Armoire ◄───► **Tall Chest**
Uses more floor space | Uses less floor space

Chaise Lounge ◄───► **Chair with Ottoman**
Space maker | Needs more room

Reach-In Closet ◄───► **Walk-In Closet**
Least space needed | More storage

One Walk-In Closet ◄───► **His and Her Closets**
Only if you can share | More space needed

Bigger Bedroom ◄───► **Bigger Dressing Room**
Limited storage space | Greater storage space

Night Owl
A Bedtime Story

HANG TIMES

Imagine the perfect closet, softly lit, and a chair for pondering. Of course, it's 3AM and you're examining your clothes instead of really sleeping!

SOME OF YOU CAN BE LULLED to sleep with soft music, warm tea, or a lengthy book. Not you Night Owls! There is so much going on in your mind that you cannot simmer down to rest. And if you do, you just start thinking about all you have to do tomorrow, or what you did not get done today.

You know there is no sense just lying in bed when you're wide awake. So you probably get up and head elsewhere (if space permits) to read, watch TV, or—heaven forbid—start working again. Stop for a moment and ponder this: if you get up, it might be hours before you get back into bed.

Lighting is the important element for Night Owl design. You need to be able to move around the room

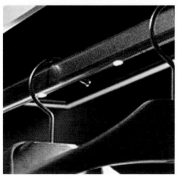

NIGHT LIGHTS

Instead of a glaring nightlight, how about an LED glow over the hanging rod in your closet? It allows you to see details without the brightness of incandescent bulbs .

quietly without disturbing your partner. The simple solution is a good flashlight on hand, but you could easily install dimmers on the nearest lamps, or even a motion detector or nightlight in the next room, to illuminate the way to that comfortable chair and ottoman. Call it your *thinking space*.

A good Night Owl plans ahead, and subtle differences to your room can help those 2AM roamings. If you have already minimized the unnecessary furniture in your bedroom with built-ins, there is no chance of bumping into the sharp corners of that bureau, or crashing into the armoire. They have gone. In their place are softer, more rounded furnishings allowing you to pad around without injury.

As long as you're awake, you could head into your closet and start sorting out your clothes, or better yet, plan your outfits for the next few days. This is a good, quiet, and necessary Right-Sizing project, but it does require a walk-in closet, or dressing room with subtle lighting design, and a good chair for pondering your wardrobe.

Somehow, in the middle of the night, you can admire your home in a special way. There is no noise, and the silence even extends to the soft, cushy carpet underfoot. Maybe it really *is* time to try sleep again. Head back to your bedroom. At last, that truly comfortable bed lures you in, and before you know it, you are fast asleep. ●

NIGHT HEARTED

It might be difficult to leave this opulent bed, but the soft chair beckons. The light, on a dimmer, is just right for your nightly amble around the house.

Bedroom Mate

All Together Now

WHILE YOU MAY lead separate, busy lives during the day, one place you do have a meeting of the minds at night is in your bedroom. Hopefully the two of you are of like minds when it comes to furnishing the room, as well as how the space needs to function. You may feel like it is your own nest you never want to leave, while your Bedroom Mate thinks it is great to just crash and watch movies. As long as this in-bed film festival does not involve popcorn, you should be okay.

Today's bedrooms involve too many choices. What size bed is comfortable for you both? Can you agree on the softness or firmness of the mattress? Do you like your sheets tucked in or laying loose? He likes carpeting and you like bare wooden floors. You really want a romantic canopy bed, and your companion has her eye on a shaped sleigh bed. The list goes on and on. Bigger battles have been fought over lesser issues. Let's agree that you *will* resolve all this and find peace, because you have not even begun to consider divvying up the closet space!

DUAL FUNCTION

This light and airy bed is a comfortable width, making it perfect for sharing. The headboard provides great support for reading or watching TV. Make sure the mattress is one you both like.

Bedrooms today are going through another change in size. This gives a lot of fuel to the design fire, and how this room can be used. Maybe you use this area to exercise in private? Of course, the two of you will never admit it, but this is also your second-favorite dining space!

As the bedroom takes on more duties, you have to reconcile the space you have versus the space you need. What is most important to you both?

We then get into the touchy area of clothes and shoe storage. It would be nice if you could convert some space into a dressing room—or two larger closets—but that might not be possible. Remember to take a look at who has the most stuff and then take into account how you store these possessions. If shoes are your thing, then what does he or she have in equal proportion? Is it bulky sweaters or hanging garments?

If things have come to blows over whose sneakers take precedence, then it's time to hire a professional organizer as a mediator of closet space. They are able to perform miracles in transforming both your clothing needs, and your partner's, into what really fits.

Perhaps it's not necessary to store all your clothes in your current closet arrangement. Consider storing out-of-season garments at your dry cleaner, if he offers this service, or even renting an outside storage closet. The war of the clothes can be resolved, and peace can return to the bedroom. ●

DIVIDING LINE

A great master chest can give both of you ample storage, and also be the base for your flat screen TV.

GUEST APPEARANCES

Take some advice from the experts. Think about twin beds for your guests. Look in the youth area of furniture stores for great values and styles.

Kid Smarts

SLEEPOVER

A daybed over a trundle bed is the perfect solution for a smaller child's room. It allows friends to stay the night.

DON'T WE ALL NEED A PLACE of our own? This certainly applies to children, no matter their age. If you are like most parents, the challenge is how to provide an enjoyable environment in which your kids can grow. Whether sleeping, playing, studying, or just hanging out, youngsters spend a lot of time in their room.

One problem to tackle upfront is that of space. In today's home, the master bedroom has grown in size, while children's rooms have shrunk. You might have a hard time fitting in a bed, dresser, chair, and desk (or even a changing table), while still having the necessary floor space for lounging. Luckily, there are new, space-saving designs, such as storage headboards, under-bed storage drawers, and loft beds, which are efficient pieces for cramped quarters. Look for youth furniture collections with pieces that can be added as your child grows.

The bed is the main focus of any bedroom. Opt for timeless design rather than the theme of the moment. Kids tend to outgrow everything somewhat quickly—even their furniture—and their tastes change, too. Will that bunk bed really work for a cool teenager? With careful planning, whatever bed you choose should serve

KID'S WORLD

Be sure to allow enough floor space in your child's room to accommodate one or two good friends for playing or just giggling.

READING IN BED

This headboard lets he or she read in bed comfortably, and saves space by storing books and toys against the wall, within easy reach.

through several stages of childhood.

Safety is a real concern. Carefully read the labels on children's furniture. The bed should be strong and stable, even for the best jumping game. To avoid a potential tip-over, bookcases should not be overloaded with books and toys. For extra safety, attach shelving units to the walls. Check for safety hinges on toy chests to prevent pinching little fingers. The U.S. Consumer Product Safety Commission (www.cpsc.gov) has further information.

It's amazing how much stuff little kids collect, and it never seems to stop. Coping with storage is as continual a battle as cleaning up after that toddler or teen. Think of how much space you might need, then double that amount. Toys, games, dolls, stuffed animals—not to mention those Barbies and superhero action figures with their minuscule accessories—give way to video games, CD players, and computers, plus wire management and accessory products. The good news is that a myriad of storage bins and drawers provide the answer, no matter who picks up the mess and clutter.

Probably you? ●

Measuring Up
Bedroom Dimension Guide

How much space do you really need to Right-Size your bedroom? Each drawing below shows a typical bedroom layout, with four different bed configurations. Use the indicated minimum spaces, or more, around the bed for comfort and usability.

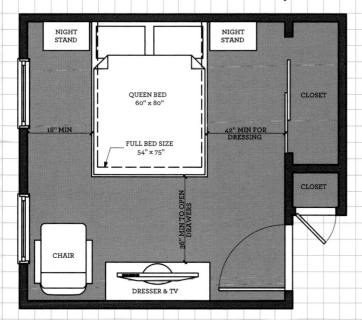

ADULT BEDROOM WITH QUEEN BED

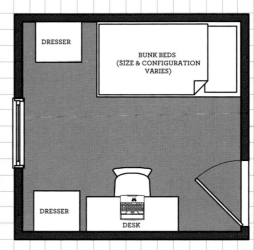

SHARED BEDROOM WITH BUNK BEDS

GENERAL TIPS:

- Bedside cabinets, rather than tables, offer more storage options
- Be sure you have room to open closet doors and drawers
- Leave enough space between bed and closet to dress comfortably
- Round is a better shape between twin beds—no corners
- A floor lamp next to your favorite chair or chaise takes up less space than an extra table and lamp

- Built-ins can eliminate furniture and make room for a bigger bed
- Mounting the TV on the wall makes for more floor space
- Bedside lamps mounted on the wall mean more room on your nightstand
- When planning space for your bed, don't forget to include dimensions of the headboard and footboard
- A mirror on the inside of the bedroom entry door saves wall space
- Remember the 50/25/25 percent rule of storage space
- Bunk bed components offer different combinations for work and sleep

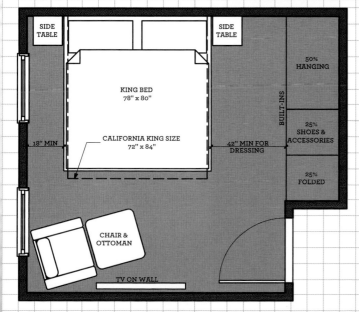

MODIFIED ADULT BEDROOM WITH KING BED

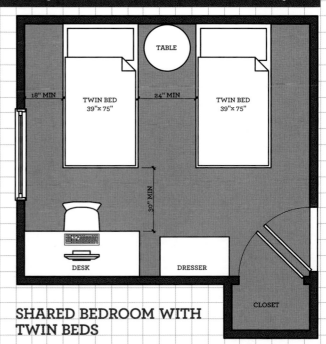

SHARED BEDROOM WITH TWIN BEDS

Road Warrior
Homing Instincts

OME AGAIN? IT'S A BIT confusing sometimes to remember exactly where you are. If this is the case, then you are a Road Warrior, and you're happy to be home once more.

Travel is no longer glamorous. Those long lines at the airport, the tedious driving through unfamiliar territory, hurried meals, and most of all, tossing and turning in a strange bed, all make business travel today frustrating. The latter is no longer the most sensitive issue.

During your last trip, you slept very well. Maybe you longed for your own familiar things around you. After all, a hotel is no place like home.

However, all those nights on the road have taught you the importance of true comfort. You discovered you really don't need chocolates on your pillow or a handy minibar to create that five-star experience in your own bedroom. What were the ingredients that made those rooms so special?

The bed you enjoyed, with the "just right," well-tested mattress and firm pillows is your most important welcome on the road. Your favorite bedside reading is nearby, nestled next to the ever-present alarm clock or radio, all watched over by an excellent lamp with just enough wattage. Now you can really appreciate a light that can be turned on and off without getting out of bed!

And then there may be the chance to relax in a comfortable chair—not that hard, straight-backed one you have back home.

PACKING IT IN
The packing island is a highly useful piece of furniture, combining handy storage with a practical, flat folding surface.

SLEEP-IN LUXURY
Even the cat recognizes the pleasures of a great bed. Like a luxury hotel bed, this one is hard to leave in the early morning hours.

That chair was better for clothes than for you.

Call them lessons from the road. One thing you learned is to make sure you have a large, flat surface (as you had in your hotel room) that lets you work comfortably on your laptop, or spread out your papers at home. Maybe create some open space for a quick in-room workout. Admit you like having all amenities within steps of your plush bed. And hide away those clothes!

Your own form of storage, whether a chest of drawers or a convenient, well-appointed closet where everything is in order for the next trip, shows that you are indeed home again. You can look forward to a restful night in your own comfortable setting.

With efficient, discreet clothes storage, room to work, and electronic controls within reach, your bedroom will not only be a place for you to get some work done, but will also keep your tired, Road Warrior self focused on the serious business of sleeping. ●

TAKE IT AWAY

Running out with no time to search for your clothes? Hang them on this handy clothes rod in your closet, the day before you leave.

WELL-SUITED

A softly-lit closet is a boon to the Road Warrior. A well-organized space makes leaving almost trouble-free.

Secret Napper

The Surreptitious Sleeper

READY FOR BED

Having a comfy bed ready for you is the best part of secret napping. Pull back that crisp duvet and sink right in for a restorative sleep.

F COURSE, NO ONE should ever know that you are a Secret Napper. You are careful to hide all evidence of your ritual. The bed is remade, the curtains are opened, the shades are rolled up, and the sleep is wiped from your eyes. And the best part of your stealthy snooze is that you emerge refreshed.

But what about the environment that helps you achieve this restful habit? Have you learned over time exactly what you need to make your bedroom, or wherever you nap, a pleasant retreat?

First is the issue of where you sleep. It may or may not be your bed. You might consider a comfortable chaise, cozy chair and ottoman, or cushy sofa better alternatives for those 40 winks. Kick off those shoes, put your feet up, and snuggle up with a warm, soft throw.

If your bed is a mid-afternoon destination, then those cool luxurious sheets invite you to unwind. Apply the "Goldilocks" test to where you rest your head: the pillows must be perfect—not too hard and not too soft.

Your surroundings are important as well. To achieve real peace and quiet, you need to reduce noise and light. The latter can be handled with window coverings, whether blinds, shades, or well-lined draperies. Noise reduction can be accomplished with plush, wall to wall carpeting, or a large, thick rug to soak up ambient sound. Keep some earplugs handy just in case.

Don't forget—the temperature of your space is crucial for complete comfort. Does the ceiling fan need to be turned on? Or the air conditioner set on low, a perfect white sound purring in the background?

If it feels just right, you are ready for that reinvigorating siesta. And who's to ever know? ●

ONE-NIGHT STAND

A bedside table is a great place to hide your sleeping mask and earplugs.

DAY DREAMER

When the urge to snooze hits, having a welcoming chair and ottoman close by is the answer.

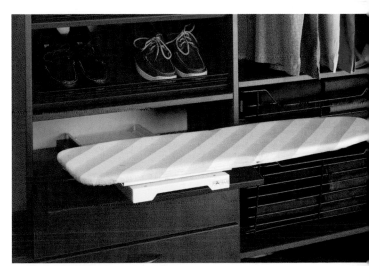

BEST PRESSED

You forgot to take off all your clothes before you slept. Pull out that handy ironing board hiding in the closet to handle the wrinkles.

Guest Smarts

NO TIME LIKE THE PRESENT TO REEVALUATE the guest room. When did you last pay any attention to your guest accommodations? Was it when you were stripping the bedding after the last visitor? Do you use this room for other purposes, blithely ignoring what a guest will encounter? Will those you invited feel you created a special place for them? (*Uninvited* guests are a whole different story!)

Above all, you want your company to feel welcome in a comfortable and self-sufficient setting. Comfort means space, so empty out some of the stuff you have accumulated there, and clear out a couple of drawers as well. A completely empty closet is too much to ask,

SUITE SETUP

The perfect guest room is comfortable, uncluttered, and welcoming. Start with a great bed, quality bedding, and extra space for when you need it.

especially if this is also your home office, but at least clear out one or two feet of hanging space, and provide four or five hangers. An alternate suggestion for hanging clothes is an over-the-door hook.

Maybe it's time for *you* to spend a night in the guest room—and take a pad and pen for notes. The comfort minimum is a non-saggy mattress, fresh bedding, a choice of pillows,

SLEEPER HIT

If room for a bed is an issue, consider a sleeper sofa. The latest sleepers can be a most restful experience, save space, and create seating.

and extra blankets. How about a place to put a suitcase while your guest is unpacking, or throughout their stay? Is there a good bedside light? You might want to add an illuminated alarm clock or clock radio to that hospitality list. Do you find there are privacy issues when sleeping in this room? Window coverings or shades not only offer privacy, but also light control.

Okay, you have now advanced beyond the pared-down look of an inexpensive motel. There's no need to provide the luxuries of a five-star hotel, but if the guest room is not connected to a bathroom, provide a one-size-fits-all robe and disposable slippers to make that trip down the hall less awkward.

Finally, keep your pets from being unwanted visitors in the bedroom during your guest's stay.

Now everything is in order, and you can play the fabulous host. ●

Now It's Your Turn

Right-Sizing *Your* Bedroom

N O MATTER THE SIZE, THERE NEVER SEEMS TO BE
enough room for all your needs and wants. Smaller bedrooms
provide their own interesting design challenges, while larger
ones offer equally demanding opportunities to function better.
If you have already completed the "Sleeping Style Audit" and
"Redesign Plan For The Bedroom," you should be clearer about your needs versus
your wants. Let's look at how to achieve that special bedroom of your dreams
within the space you have. ●

Freestanding Furniture versus Built-In Furniture

RETHINK FURNITURE/ CLOSET COMBO

Organizing the closet will undoubtedly produce more space. Also, use the bed itself to create more storage. The space under the bed instead of a trundle will give you folding space for clothes. Or think vertically—how about a bunk bed with the lower area for storage?

RESULT:
More features in same space

THINK BUILT-IN FURNITURE ONLY

In a smaller bedroom, there is usually a lot of furniture crammed into tiny space. Create a more satisfying sleeping experience by getting rid of some furniture, and building storage into the closet or an existing armoire. You can make the room seem bigger without all the clutter.

RESULT:
More space created

THINK FURNITURE ONLY

The newer generations of furniture can multi-task nicely. Many pieces come with hidden storage—the chair that becomes a single bed, the bench that hides bulky storage, the bed that has a small closet integrated into its design. Look around for innovative pieces that work hard and store well.

RESULT:
Allows more space

8

Where You Work

"Heigh-ho, Heigh-ho, it's off to work we go!" *Most of us don't start the day singing this little ditty, but if you are among the many now working at home, you might start doing so because you have no commute.*

REMEMBER WHEN A HOME OFFICE WAS JUST FOR show, or even a place at the end of a kitchen counter? In the history of home design, it wasn't all that long ago that the word *office* referred to the study. The computer has changed how, when, and where we work at home. With wireless available in most areas, we now have the option to choose *where* we work as well.

This new reality of our roller coaster economy has brought more of us home to work part-time, or even full-time. Some of us have started businesses in unused corners of the home. (Is there really such a things as unused corners?) Others, including our young or college-aged children, bring work home. The only occupants who don't seem to be working are our pets.

Since our homes were not designed to be workplaces, finding a place to comfortably work or study at our computers can be a challenge. There is seldom an empty room not already used for another purpose. How many of us find ourselves improvising a workspace in the guest room, former child's room, laundry area, dining room, or even our bedroom? What about the attic or a portion of the basement? Other creative locations include the space under the stairs, a large walk-in closet, or a large loft balcony. No space is sacred. What room can we afford to give up?

Most of us start small, but when we factor in the need for storage as well as workspace, we've enlarged our office space considerably. Whatever space we think we need, should be doubled. Magazines show images of impeccable, tiny spaces for a home office, but the question is, who really works there—or could? It is time to get real.

The work-at-home trend is not going away any time soon, especially with a commute reduced to less than a minute. Making room for a successful, functional workplace is another part of the *Right Sizing Your Home* process.

BUSINESS CASUAL

Kick off your shoes and settle into your new office with a view. Before you do, plan your workspace with the best furniture and equipment.

Working Style Audit

Select the working style that best reflects you. Then follow the tips below for creating more space and order, suited to that style.

ARE YOU A TELECOMMUTER?

- ○ Need a workspace, but not on a daily basis
- ○ Office should be very functional
- ○ Need to be able to lock away files

TIPS:

- Plan on an office space that multitasks as another, seldom-used room
- Divide workspace into maximum desk and minimum storage
- Create a space for sorting and organizing materials, and repacking
- Use a secure filing system or a closet that locks, if sharing the space

ARE YOU A SELF EMPLOYEE?

- ○ Want to create a space for creativity
- ○ Office needs to be fashionable
- ○ Need light and noise control

TIPS:

- Plan on using maximum space in the room, or rededicate the entire space to a home office
- Desk area should have easy access to parallel counter space
- Create a space for rolling carts for storing ongoing projects
- Use one wall for an ideas board, as inspiration

ARE YOU AN OFFICE SHARER?

- ○ Office space is shared by more than one
- ○ Office needs to be double-duty
- ○ This office never sleeps

TIPS:

- Plan on a large counter space for spreading out projects
- Have separate, locked storage for each user, but have a common printer
- Desk space needs to have room for two chairs
- Create noise control for late-night inspiration

ARE YOU A PART-TIME BOSS?

- ○ Want a duplicate of the office, at home
- ○ Workspace should be elegant
- ○ Need storage invisible from workspace

TIPS:

- Plan on converting an unused room into a home office
- Need a well-designed desk and status furniture in a dedicated room
- Create space for sitting or small conferences
- Use a nearby closet for paper and supply storage, or invest in furniture that discreetly hides away filing

ARE YOU A HOMEWORKER?

- ○ Want a family communications center
- ○ Office does not need to be a dedicated space
- ○ Used to catch-up on work, bills, or correspondence

TIPS:

- Plan on using a convenient area in a larger room
- Maximize storage and minimize workspace
- Create space for temporary storage of work, but hide cabinets for financial records
- Use a bulletin board for family or spousal updates

Self Employee
I Am My Own Boss

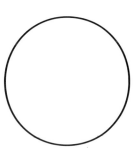

KAY, YOU'RE WORKING at home now. Was it life's bumps in the road that brought you back here? Maybe a great idea for a new business motivated you? Are you going solo after a long stretch in a companion-filled office? Or have job circumstances changed and you couldn't refuse? There could be many reasons for this relocation, and new status as a self employee.

The big challenge is how to balance your real life with your work life. While you save time and money with no commute and no need for office clothes, there are interruptions, the temptations of family life, household chores, and even pets that leave plenty of room for procrastination.

That's why having an office where you can really get work done helps separate you from the rest of your home. Go into your work zone and close that real or imaginary door.

As a Self Employee who needs to get the business rolling, you require a space that suits your personal needs, as well as your working style. Are you a "show it or stow it" kind of person? If you need your files close at hand, plan on having file storage nearby that is

THE WAY TO WORK
If your new office is visible, find furniture that complements your existing pieces, in both style and finish. This office collection is open stock so you can add more as needed.

HOME STUDY

Your rarely-used study makes the perfect new workplace. Clear out the clutter and start fresh with an ergonomic chair and desk, plus room to grow the business.

OVAL OFFICE

Convert your dining room into a daytime office, then back again for evening meals. Make sure you allow for paper and file storage elsewhere.

complementary to your desk's finish and style. This is a good way to avoid the hodgepodge pitfall many home offices fall into.

If you work better with open bins for projects, make sure the clutter does not overwhelm your workspace. A hutch over your desk, wall organizer, or bookshelves will help you establish priority storage for ongoing and backup files. Put the rest away in stacking bins or—better yet—in an organized office closet. If the materials are clearly labeled, they do not have to be "out of sight, out of mind."

Get your office equipment up to speed, too. Make sure you have an adequate power source running your printer, fax, answering machine, and postage meter at an optimal level. Include an upgraded phone line or service to meet your increased needs. Plan on keeping your new home office looking professional, but don't neglect it as a personal space as well. You're the boss! ●

Office Redesign Plan

Before you start planning to change your home office, look at the check lists below. The items you check should help guide you in assessing your space, and how it might work best for you. Use these responses to define the problems, as well as the solutions.

Reasons for making a change?
(check all that apply)
- O Entire office is too small
- O Office is shared with bedroom or other space
- O Layout is not functional
- O Lack of storage for files, paper supplies
- O Desk is outdated or unappealing
- O Privacy problems on shared computer
- O Poor lighting
- O Not enough counter space
- O Inadequate lighting or electrical outlets
- O Desktop computer is out of date
- O Nearby distractions

Who uses this room?
(check all that apply)
- O Adults
- O Older adults
- O Children
- O Guests

How is it used?
(check all that apply)
- O Working for business
- O Doing homework
- O Reading emails
- O Writing
- O Checking financial statements
- O Watching movies
- O Downloading and printing pictures
- O Gaming

What do you need to store here?
(check all that apply)
- O Business files
- O Ongoing project files
- O Expense files
- O Tax files
- O Paper supplies
- O Mailing supplies
- O Printer, computer supplies, and software
- O Checks and bank statements
- O Reference materials and books
- O Awards and plaques

What do you need for more comfort?
(check all that apply)
- O Better desk
- O More storage space
- O Adequate lighting
- O Anti-static, low pile carpeting
- O Great office chair
- O Additional counter space
- O Innovative way to hide away office
- O Improved glare control
- O Less furniture
- O More privacy
- O Soundproofing
- O Separate chair for reading
- O Wire management

Trade-Offs

As you map out a plan for Right-Sizing your home office, think about the trade-offs below. Remember to take into consideration the amount of space you really have, while weighing wants versus needs.

VERSUS

Dedicated Office Space ◄—► **Shared Office Space**	
More working space	Less working space

Computer Desk ◄————► **Recycled Traditional Desk**	
Ready to use	Needs reconfiguration

Computer Desk ◄————► **Armoire Desk**	
More workspace	Less workspace

Rolling Desk Chair ◄—► **Static Desk Chair**	
Flexible movement	Less mobility

File Cabinets ◄————► **Built-In Storage**	
Less office space	More office space

VERSUS

Locked File Storage ◄—► **Exposed Files**	
More privacy	Less privacy

Nearby Counter Space ◄—► **Dining Table**	
Closer to work site	Less convenient

Single-Use Printer ◄—► **Shared Printer**	
More convenient	Less space needed

Reach-In Closet ◄—► **Walk-In Closet**	
Least space needed	More storage

PLUGGED-IN

When you're accustomed to wireless, then working from home should offer the same convenience. Have a great chair near your writing desk for flexible computing.

Part-Time Boss

Executive Decision

YOU CAN TELL YOURSELF you're not really working at home. You just bring work home, spending evenings or even weekends catching up on business reading, paperwork, and those knotty, work-related decisions still to be made. This means you are a Part-time Boss.

Ideally you would like a miniature version of your corporate office at home, but can you devote an entire room to an office that is only used one or two nights a week? Packing up your projects at the end of a home work session does require space, even though you are equipped with a great laptop, a portable organizer, plus the latest generation of a personal digital assistant.

The biggest thing to consider as a Part-Time Boss is your desk, particularly if it's visible from other rooms. Think about how you work. Does everything have to be within arm's reach? Do you work better with your desk facing the window, the door, or the wall? Position can be everything.

Really take the time to plan your home office configuration. The effort will reward you with an efficient and personalized space for many years. Is your new desk going to overwhelm or underwhelm the room you have chosen? Are you accustomed to having a credenza close by for space to spread out files? Can the paperwork you store be part of your temporary office plan, or does

CURVE APPEAL

Handsome, contemporary cabinets on legs cleverly form the foundation for this space-saving office. The curved desk defines the work area from the rest of the room.

it have to hide away in part of the closet? Remember, here at home, keeping clutter under control is your responsibility, not your secretary's.

It will make you feel better to do a cost/value analysis of your home office investment, and treat every purchase as a business decision. Of course, you may not be the only one in this household to weigh-in with an opinion. Ask your spouse or partner about color scheme or fabric choices, as these should blend or mix well with the existing décor in nearby rooms. Decisions, decisions! ●

OUT OF SIGHT

Some office equipment is best hidden away, mostly if you occasionally work at home. Find a handsome console that efficiently provides office apparatus management.

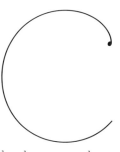

**LIGHT
WORK**

*If you have given
up part of your
bedroom to a
desk, then wake
up to something
beautiful. Select
home work
furniture that
harmonizes with
your décor and
color scheme.*

Telecommuter

Being Here or There

CONTINUING ON THE company payroll, but working from home occasionally? This makes you a Telecommuter, and you have the best of both worlds. When you feel isolated from your coworkers, or a little lonely, you can always return to the office.

The good news is that you are free to set up your home office as you please, making it less boring and more personal. Maybe the company has provided you with some, or all, of your furniture and other equipment, but they don't dictate the wall or floor color, or which picture you hang. That's your choice!

Maybe this arrangement is in a "test" stage, and you elect to keep the look functional and simple until you settle in, or in the event your company office (or company) should no longer exist.

If this is a transition, your home office needs may change. You may find working on your laptop at the dining room table gives your more freedom, and more space to spread out your papers. After all, no one is looking except you. If you didn't inherit a great office chair in your Telecommuter transition, don't use a dining room chair or old kitchen stool. They're not designed for working. Invest in the best chair you can afford. The more time you spend at your home computer, the more you need a supportive, well-designed, ergonomic chair that fits your body shape. Look for lumbar support and variable back height, head, seat, and arm rests. You may also need a tilt mechanism for reducing strain on your lower back and leg muscles. Do you want a chair that remains stationary, or one with coasters to move as you move? Finally, consider how this chair will fit into your color scheme. Now sit back and get to work! ●

FILE STYLE

If space is tight, you may not be able to store files in your home office. Think creatively about file storage, placing it near your workspace as a decorative arrangement.

BACK OFFICE

You found space in your laundry room and converted built-in cabinets into an efficient workplace. Since you only need this area part-time, the stool and storage are not a problem.

Kid Smarts

HOMEWORK STARTS EARLY IN LIFE, AND
it never seems to stop. There's no time off for good
behavior, except during summer holidays. Then there may
be assignments to complete, or even summer school.

Developing good study habits takes time and
encouragement. Creating a quiet workspace at home,
free from the distractions of TV, music, or games, is the
first order of business. Having a dedicated, practical
desk and sturdy chair makes this a more serious pursuit.
Although kids gravitate to the kitchen or family room—
where parents can keep a watchful eye on them—
ultimately having a workspace of their own is important.

Children's needs for a place to work will change as they
grow, so there is no one size to fit all. A preschooler may
like drawing, so his or her small desk or table needs rollout
paper, to feed their creativity. A grade schooler needs an
age-appropriate, durable desk with a few drawers, and
space for that first home computer.

By the time the teenage years roll around, electronics
dominate the now-enlarged desk area with not only
a computer, but a CD player, iPod, and hopefully
homework. Think about a hutch attachment for the top

DESK JOB
*Placing a desk
under the top bunk
instead of another
bed, creates a
private study area.
Expand storage
with a small file
caddy on wheels.*

**THE WRITE
STUFF**
*Add space to a
small bedroom
by thinking
vertically. A
desktop hutch adds
storage, as well as
display space.*

of the desk, to hold all the clutter
that is beginning to accumulate (or
already has). Don't forget to include
a comfortable chair for that growing
body. The hope is that your child will
concentrate and work better.

Even for the smallest tots, sizing
the furniture makes a difference.
There should be no more than 8 to
10 inches between the top of their
seated lap, and the desk or table. The
lower leg determines the correct seat
height. Measure from the floor to the
bent knees.

It's never too early for thinking
about ergonomics. A child's
workplace must be comfortable, with
enough room to accommodate their
needs. Workspace furniture must be
properly sized so your child can work
at his or her best. ●

Measuring Up
Office Dimension Guide

How much space do you really need to Right-Size your home office? Each drawing below shows a typical office layout, with four different desk configurations. Use the recommended (REC), or at least the minimum (MIN), space needed around the desk, for comfort and usability.

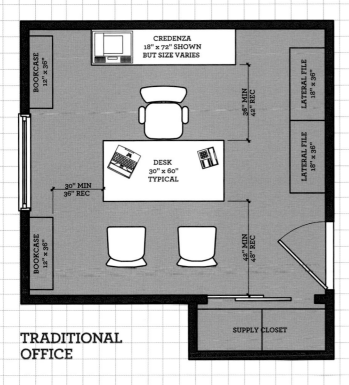

TRADITIONAL OFFICE

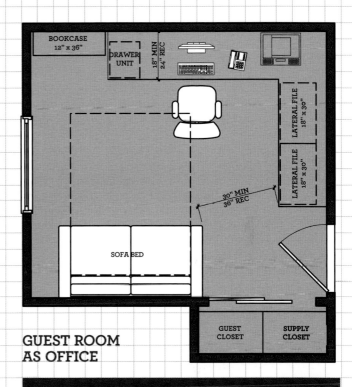

GUEST ROOM AS OFFICE

GENERAL TIPS:

- Bilateral files can be 30, 36, or 42 inches wide
- Two-drawer file cabinets can fit under desktops, or provide a convenient spot for a printer
- Use file drawers for organizing and storing supplies, not just files
- Consider your computer, printing, and networking needs when laying out your office
- Desks against walls leave more open space in the room, and are easier to keep tidy
- Bookcases can be used to separate or screen work areas
- A keyboard tray can adjust the height of the keyboard, save desktop space, or allow for a shallower desktop

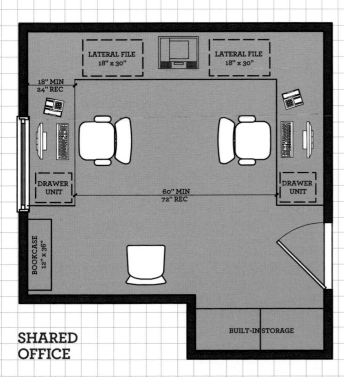

SHARED OFFICE

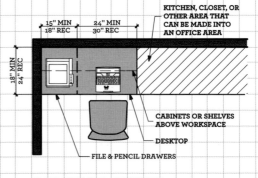

COMPACT OFFICE

KEEPING PEACE

Not many couples who live together, work together. It takes neutral territory to keep the peace. Take over a whole room, allowing enough space for both of you.

Office Sharer

Team Work

SHARING ANYTHING REQUIRES patience and tolerance, but when it comes to sharing an office, you'll need a special understanding and personal awareness to make it work. Even when sharing with someone you love, reflecting on long-term ramifications and family politics, before plunging ahead, is crucial.

There are several reasons for considering a dual work arrangement. You might share the space with an employee or a business partner, but most likely you will share the office with a family member. Ideally, use would be split between daytime and evening so that you each have an uninterrupted block of time to dedicate to your work. If both of you work the same hours, you will need to clarify printer, fax, and telephone usage to minimize distraction. A shared computer requires a more specific schedule.

Two people using one office means dividing the space into two work areas. If you need two separate desks, measure *twice*, making sure there is adequate space for both. You'll need room to spread out, to organize files, collate, and use the computer(s) and the printer. Space for storing files and supplies may or may not be equally divided, but both users need adequate room for it all.

Of course, the shared office may actually be between

parent and child, or between two children. Whatever the case, having a clear understanding of how each person works, helps make both parties more productive. It also helps in keeping arguments at a minimum.

Furniture, supplies, and equipment have been addressed, but what about lighting? If one person prefers direct lighting while they work, and the other likes a more indirect light, you can easily resolve this with a combination of well-placed task lights and non-glare ambient light.

This partnership can work on every level. And let's not forget—you can defray business costs, so be sure to keep track of all your expenses. Both of you! ●

A FAMILY AFFAIR

Call this desk the family communications center, placing it convenient to your kitchen. Everyone will have easy access for working and messaging.

EQUAL SHARES

Some home offices barely have enough space for one person to work, much less two. This Right-Sized stair landing shows you can effectively work in tandem, even in the tiniest space.

SHADY BUSINESS

Not all work happens when the light is just right. Good shades are a great office investment to help with light control and avoid glare.

Home Worker

Works for Me

SOMETIMES THE DECISION to work at home is motivated by a desire to spend more time with family. This is particularly true if you have children in preschool or an elderly parent in residence. If keeping close to home is important, become a Home Worker, especially if you know you can continue your career.

The Home Worker must be very disciplined, because babies, small children, and even pets are obvious distractions. Then there is the television, washer or dryer, and the tempting refrigerator to lure you away from your work. Babysitters, on a regular schedule, can assure consistent work time for the first problem. Locating your office further away from household enticements may help with the others.

Define the priorities of your workday, and close the door to get them done. Keep your desk free of clutter, which can also become a distraction. Making a to-do list at the end of each day, to be accomplished the next day, will help keep you on track.

Many Home Workers do not have dedicated office space, and frequently must multitask in a room that is multitasking itself. Create a way to separate your work

area from the rest of the room—perhaps a folding screen. Consider physical boundaries, such as a low bookcase, to establish your space without blocking the light.

The big question is how permanent is working at home? Is this a temporary phase of your career, stemming from family obligations or company cutbacks? Are you making a commitment to stay home on a more permanent basis? The answer will help you decide on a budget for office furniture and other equipment. You'll want to invest in the best quality you can afford. Remember, a flexible workspace can always be upgraded if your needs change. ●

DESK BOUND?

A Home Worker may need a little flexibility from time to time. This banquette is a tempting place to work—and it's near the coffeemaker!

CLOSET SHOW

When you need a small workplace, think about a closet area. Place storage on shelves above your work surface. Close the door when finished.

Guest Smarts

THESE DAYS, THE PERFECT GUEST ROOM IS
almost as rare as the perfect guest. The truth is the
dedicated spare room, just waiting for the infrequent
overnight visitor, is a thing of the past. Most of us don't
have the luxury of separate, interior real estate. More
than likely, this room is doing double duty as full-time
home office and part-time guest quarters.

There are clever solutions for space saving, and
temporary sleeping arrangements in this double-duty
room. The sleeper sofa, once the subject of a tale of
nighttime tossing and turning, has evolved into a softer
and sounder night's sleep on what almost feels like a
real bed. No more nasty bar in the middle of your back!
When shopping for a convertible sofa, open it up and
try it out for comfort. The goal here is to find a piece of
furniture that sleeps as well as it sits!

An old-time, sleep-over solution, such as the Murphy

SLEEP ON

*Who would
imagine that this
cushy sofa hides a
most comfy bed?
Test it out before
inviting a guest,
however.*

HIDE &
SLEEP

*When this Zoom-
Room bed is
hidden behind the
entertainment unit,
it is truly invisible.
Taking up little
additional space, it
pulls out very easily.*

bed, literally pulled down from the
wall to create an instant bedroom.
Such old models meant giving up
floor and wall space. The latest
generation of pull-down beds offers
a selection of upgraded mattresses,
and other accessories, such as
built-in lighting, plus the ability to
attach artwork or decoration to the
wall that hides the bed.

A wonderfully inventive way to
accommodate occasional guests is
the Zoom-Room. It has a retractable
mattress and frame that hide
behind a bookcase or entertainment
unit. No one is the wiser about the
bed's location, until you reveal the
secret. Presto chango, you have a
part-time guest room.

Of course there might come a
time you claim you have no spare
bed at all. Oh, but you wouldn't do
that! Would you? ●

Now It's Your Turn

Right-Sizing *Your* Office

YOU HAVE FOUND THE PERFECT SPOT FOR YOUR NEW home office, but before you can move in, you need to create a layout that suits your work style. Refer to your results from the "Working Style Audit" and the "Office Redesign Plan." Look at how many supplies you need on hand, and what you need to store. The goal is to make this workspace more functional and less cluttered. Then the rest is up to you. ●

Freestanding Desk versus Built-In Desk

THINK FREESTANDING, BUILT-IN COMBO	**RETHINK FREESTANDING DESK**	**THINK BUILT-IN DESK ONLY**
If space permits, this layout can give you the best of both worlds. You can enjoy the flexibility of moving the furniture, while maximizing your additional workspace. Try to coordinate finishes to blend together, if not match.	*This arrangement allows you the flexibility to change your mind about your office layout. If the desk is not against a wall, buy one with a finished back before free-floating it in the middle of the room. Open stock furniture allows you to add pieces later.*	*Make the most of a tiny space with this setup. Built-in cabinets can be designed to customize your workspace to suit your personal needs. You can also adjust the height of your desktop counter to a higher or lower comfort level to fit your chair.*
RESULT: *More features in same space*	**RESULT:** *Allows more flexible space*	**RESULT:** *More space created*

Where You Clean & Store

Face it—one of your favorite Peanuts characters is Pigpen. *Take a good look at your laundry room, open your linen closet, or the cabinet under the kitchen sink, or the sideboard in your dining room, and you'll see his subtle influence. Things fall out because, despite your best intentions to organize, you simply haven't gotten around to it. Of course, you would never admit this in polite company, but there's still a little Pigpen inside each of us.*

I **KNOW ABOUT THESE PROBLEMS FIRST HAND. WHILE** writing this book, I have been forced to ignore a family of dust bunnies who have taken up residence in my home...and they seem to be multiplying as I write! In reality I'm a neat person, so I know this isn't a permanent infestation.

For most of us, our good intentions get in the way of our actions. Do you really keep up with the laundry? How about organizing your ever-growing collections of linens, china, antiques, etc.? Do out-of-season clothing or supplies overwhelm you? Do you have a dedicated space for your pet's provisions? If you don't have a broom closet, where do your cleaning materials and equipment, such as vacuum and accessories, reside? And do they live together?

Whether you live in a tiny home or a mega-mansion, it doesn't matter. How you use available storage to contain your belongings is what matters. No question about it—everyone needs more storage. The big question is how do you handle this problem?

Are you a stow-away person (out of sight, out of mind) or a show-off (everything on display)? Either alternative requires discipline and a sense of purpose. Too many things on view add to the feeling of clutter, and cramming cabinets or closets to their limit just means the clutter is hidden.

This chapter takes a look at the messy areas of the house, most of which you don't want exposed to the light of day. It's easy to comment on this dilemma, but not so easy to create room for display as well as storage, and even more difficult to maintain it.

Whether it's a dedicated laundry room or an area for your accumulations, take a moment or two to reexamine these possessions, and Right-Size now.

TAILORED TO FIT

This ingenious china cabinet offers four solutions in one: a closed display for a collection, and three storage configurations— the most clever being hidden hangers for linens, tucked in the cabinet back.

Cleaning & Storing Style Audit

Select the cleaning and storing style that best describes you.
Then follow the tips below to help you better maintain and organize your home.

ARE YOU A PET LOVER?

○ Know there are no bad pets, just humans who don't understand
○ Love that your pet is warming your favorite chair while you work
○ Look forward to that little lick or purr at the end of the day

TIPS:

- Create space near entryway for leashes, raingear, etc. to save scurrying around for them when urgency is key; towels here prevent wet, muddy paw prints
- Locate grooming supplies under the sink, or near the tub or shower, where pets are bathed; always keep separate from human supplies
- To protect pets *and* older adults or children, make sure pet pillows or cushions placed near your relaxing area are not in a traffic zone
- Use a pullout garbage pail with lid (some have wheels) to store dry food away from pets; keep treats and canned food in a pantry if possible

ARE YOU A NEAT NIK?

○ Everything should have its own place
○ Can't help rearranging other people's things
○ Love to organize possessions

TIPS:

- Use bins or baskets to keep papers, magazines, or newspapers tidy until you can organize them
- Keep items used most often easily visible; this applies to kitchen items, china, glassware, clothes, shoes, and bed linens
- Sort clothes in your closet by color; make a chart of best accessories for each color, and their stored location
- Arrange herbs and spices alphabetically; note purchase date on the bottom of these, and anything perishable, to assure freshness

ARE YOU A STOW AWAYER?

○ See closets as endless space for storing
○ Have not visited the bottom or back of the closet in ages
○ Love the hunting and gathering part; hate the storing

TIPS:

- Organize one closet or cabinet at a time using the "One-Two-Three Method" (see Step #3, page 28); store similar items together so they can be easily located
- Make *only* temporary use of found space—under stairs, beds, and even some chairs
- Reward yourself with a closet redesign to maximize existing space; keep all items within easy reach
- To store seasonal items, use stackable plastic, lidded, or cardboard containers, or metal storage baskets, well labeled

ARE YOU A FAMILY LAUNDERER?

○ Know emergency destaining tricks without referring to a chart
○ Realize that laundry is never really done
○ Want to train other family members to assume this role

TIPS:

- Gain control of weekly laundry by assigning hampers for each family member, placed wherever you know they will be used (closets, bathrooms, etc.)
- Apply a stagger system; use the time between wash and dry cycles on more rewarding activities, making sure you can hear the buzzer
- Use an adequate surface for sorting and folding; sort by user as you fold
- If squeezed for space, keep your iron and board in a nearby closet; it's best to locate your ironing area and paraphernalia in the laundry room

ARE YOU AN ARDENT COLLECTOR?

○ Believe that if one is good, twelve are better
○ Like to show off your collection(s)
○ Never saw multiples of anything that you didn't like

TIPS:

- Create an inventory of your collection and update it as it grows; periodically weed through to avoid duplication; recycle/resell pieces you don't want or like
- Allow adequate space to display at least part of your collection; swap out items periodically so you can enjoy all pieces
- Set aside space for maintenance; learn proper care for antique or fragile items, as well as wine storage needs (such as rotating bottles, etc.)
- Designate a dust-free storage area to avoid cleaning and handling fragile items; space should be inaccessible to younger children or pets

CLOTHES CASE

These modular closet units allow instant organizing, and can be modified to accommodate your selections of hanging and folded clothes. Everything becomes easy to reach and stores without cramming.

Neat Nik
Life in Order

YOU KNOW THAT everything should be in its place, and that there should be a place for everything. This isn't just a theory for the Neat Nik, it's a way of life. you work hard to take control of your possessions, and spend as much time weeding out as you do acquiring.

When sorting smaller possessions, such as kitchen utensils, you tend to organize by size or use. You're particularly pleased with your European-style dishwasher; it lets you indulge your orderly tendencies by giving single forks or knives their own slots. Some might find this a bit compulsive, but you really love not mixing up the flatware in those all-inclusive baskets!

Your goal is to make sure everything can be easily

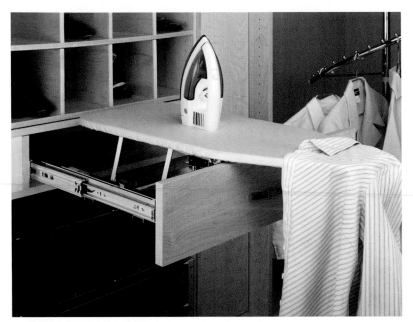

MEET THE PRESS

Having a small iron and ironing board included in your closet may seem like a luxury—until you use it. Then it quickly becomes a necessity.

FILING SYSTEM

No more kitchen clutter for you! With divided inserts inside your main drawers, utensils, knives, and scissors will find a home of their own.

seen and reached. While many people might have a more casual approach to glass-fronted kitchen cabinets, you excel in a stricter philosophy—showing off your sense of order with neatly stacked plates and well-arranged glassware. No errant soup cans or a jumble of cereal boxes. The same applies to the bathroom, where you've worked out a filing system for medicines and cosmetics. Nothing is out-of-sight and never gets lost in the back of a cupboard.

Your clothes closet reflects your fine-tuned organization. You'd never think of storing summer and winter clothes together. After all, seasonal changes give you an opportunity to sort clothing into piles for storing, donating, or tossing. The same applies to your shoes. Those worn most often have prime real estate on the shoe shelf, while those worn less frequently are stored in clearly labeled—maybe even *clear*—boxes. Scarves and gloves, a bane for the disorganized, are certainly not stuffed into jacket pockets or purses. Gloves are paired and scarves are neatly folded, tucked into drawers or plastic boxes.

Sounds like a full-fledged personal organizer like you doesn't need or desire Right-Sizing, but you're an adventurer, always on the lookout. Your frontier is a storage and organization store, where you can discover the ever-changing new products on the market that will do a better job: hanging caddies or pull-down shelves to help manage clothes; new, air-tight containers to prolong the life of foods and spices; built-in cosmetic caddies, and the like. You find ideas in home design magazines or even in retail store displays—like how to find the hidden potential in the art of folding versus hanging.

As you always say, never miss an opportunity to get sorted! ●

Cleaning & Storing Redesign Plan

Before you start planning to change any cleaning/storage areas of your home, look at the lists below. The items you check should help guide you in assessing your space, and how it might work best for you. Use these responses to define the problems, as well as the solutions.

Reasons for making a change?
(check all that apply)
- Room too small
- Closet too small or inadequate
- Need a mudroom
- Poor cabinet storage accessories
- Need better storage management
- No storage for dirty clothes
- No room for brooms and mops
- No place for collections
- Flooring is difficult to maintain
- Sink is non-existent or needs replacing
- Lack space to sort or fold clothes
- Old/inefficient appliances
- No room for ironing

Who uses this room?
(check all that apply)
- Adults
- Older adults
- Children
- Guests
- Pets

How is it used?
(check all that apply)
- Laundry
- Ironing
- Coat storage
- Clothes/shoes storage
- Seasonal storage
- Toy/game storage
- Grooming pets
- Feeding pets
- Storing collections

What do you need to store here?
(check all that apply)
- Bulk paper supplies
- Extra canned/packaged foods
- Vacuum cleaner
- Cleaning supplies
- Games and toys
- Clothes
- Coats and outerwear
- Pet grooming supplies
- Pet food

- Wine and spirits
- Water and other beverages
- Health and beauty aids

What do you need for more comfort?
(check all that apply)
- Adequate closet space
- Alternate storage space
- More workspace
- Better cabinet organization
- Laundry convenient to clothes storage
- Broom closet or cleaning pantry
- Pet supply storage
- Room for collections
- Multifunctional sink
- Dedicated mudroom
- Ergonomic vacuum cleaner
- Easy-clean surfaces

Trade-Offs

As you map out a plan for Right-Sizing your cleaning or storage areas, think about the trade-offs below. Remember to take into consideration the amount of space you really have, while weighing wants versus needs.

VERSUS

Separate Laundry Room ←→ **Built-In Stackables**
Need more space / Space saver

Laundry Near Dressing Area ←→ **Laundry Elsewhere**
More convenient / Less convenient

Ironing in Laundry ←→ **Ironing in Closet**
More space needed / Flexibility for touchups

Deep Laundry Sink ←→ **Wide Laundry Sink**
Space saver / Uses more space

Sink in Laundry ←→ **No Laundry Sink**
Space for hand-washing / More space in laundry

VERSUS

Double Bowl Sink ←→ **Utility Sink with Drainboard**
Uses more space / Adds work space

Broom Closet ←→ **Cleaning Pantry**
Limited storage capacity / Flexible storage space

Built-In Storage ←→ **Freestanding Storage**
Uses less space / Uses more space

Built-In Recycling Center ←→ **Freestanding Center**
Space saver / Uses more space

LAUNDRY BOOSTER

This laundry is too good-looking to be hidden away. The secret is discreet cabinets, and baskets that hold detergents, bleach, and supplies out of sight.

Family Launderer

Organized Labor

HERE WAS A TIME WHEN THIS space was called the utility room, filled with machines that looked like weapons of torture. That was quite a few yesterdays ago. Today's well-planned laundry room, with convenient storage and the latest appliances, turns washing clothes into a pleasure. Who are we kidding? Laundry is a chore!

The average family generates between six and eight loads of laundry each week, so whether you like this activity or not, someone has to do it. No hand wringers or scrub boards these days (how were they used anyway?).

Modern machines are so advanced they can calculate how dirty the clothes are and adjust the amount of detergent needed. Dryers are intuitive as well, and both appliances are energy efficient and less expensive to operate than older versions.

If you are the primary launderer, you should select machines with the features you really need. Among them are quick wash, rinse/hold, pre-wash, steam clean, and various settings for an assortment of fabric types. Since there may be some secondary users of these machines, they need to be easy to operate, even when the "Use and Care" books are nowhere to be found.

Many machines now offer a lock feature to prevent tiny fingers from pushing buttons.

The number of people in your household, and your laundry habits, determine what machine capacity is required. If space is tight, consider a stackable, front-loading version over the traditional side-by-side appliances. For very small homes, there are combination washer/dryers available, but beware—the limited capacity and long washing/drying cycles may be deterrents.

Laundry rooms are also no longer relegated to a corner of the cellar. Lately, home builders have been listening to their female customers, and are moving the laundry room upstairs—or nearer to the bedroom—where dirty clothes seem to breed. If your home didn't come with a laundry near the bedroom, juggling closet space or ceding bathroom square footage

WASH AND WEAR

Plan on having a sink near your washer and dryer. It doesn't have to be large. It's great for presoaking as well as drip-drying.

COLOR WASH

Give your laundry room a little personality with colorful cabinets that hide all the necessities for clean clothes. As a result, color makes this room less ordinary.

may achieve a good solution. You'll never have to haul baskets up and down stairs again!

Some homes may not have space for a dedicated laundry room, so the mudroom does double duty. In other cases, the space may be shared with crafting or gift-wrapping activities, or even a mini-office. Units located in the kitchen are handy, and may be hidden behind special cabinet doors.

Important questions to ponder if you don't have a dedicated laundry space: Where will dirty clothes be stored and sorted? Where will the iron and ironing board be used and stored? Where will you soak or pretreat stains? Where will the detergents, bleaches, and other necessary supplies hide when not in use?

While doing the laundry has become a much easier process, until clothes emerge from the machine sorted and folded, someone will still need to be in a management position. Probably you. ●

**DOGGIE
DOOR**

*Even Rover
deserves some
liquid refreshment
after returning
home from a run.
Keep a bowl handy
to the door, as well
as some treats and
his leash.*

Pet Lover

Animal Attraction

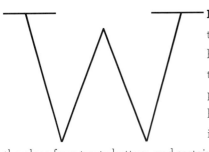

WHO KNOWS the Pet Lover's home better than the family pet? After all, he or she has investigated the place from top to bottom, and certainly knows which chairs or sofas are the most comfortable. To find out which window sills have perfect light in the middle of the day, ask your cat. The dog is the expert as to the snuggest bed in the house—and how to hop on and off leaving only the slightest trace. It's all in a day's work since this really is their "day job." After all, they're family, and somebody has to assume responsibility for keeping comfort standards up to par!

Like your two-legged family members, your animals need their own space for bathing, sleeping, relaxing, working (like barking at squirrels or neighborhood dogs), or playing. Cats, we mustn't forget, do prefer their own toilet. Of course all pets need grooming equipment, plus ample supplies of treats, food (cans, kibble, or both), and dishes for water and food. How quickly they learn where that food is stored!

Your pet's special area depends on the size and design of your home. Some lucky animals have their bowls and food supply located in the family kitchen. Others find themselves munching in the mudroom or laundry room, where there may be more convenient open space, and easier-to-maintain surfaces. Cats may try to claim an area of the countertop, but most have accepted their own part of the floor.

Areas for grooming take on their own set of requirements. Some animals of the feline persuasion declare themselves to be self-cleaning. Dogs, however, need their own beauty parlor, depending on breed and size. Make room for pet shampoos, nail clippers, towels, and the like wherever you shampoo the dog. A deep, single bowl sink, with a slip-resistant mat on the bottom, can easily serve as Fido's tub, if he's not much more than twenty pounds. Other pets might surrender to a tub bath or shower—with reservations, of course. If they love water, you're lucky.

For many, the mudroom is now the main entry to the house, so dog gear has found its way there too. It makes sense to store leads and rain/snow apparel near the door where pets come and go, much like the drop zone you might have for keys or recharging devices. A small wall cabinet or lidded stool works well as an accessories center. Make room for towels too, as well as hooks to hang them on when damp after a rainy walk.

The Right-Sizing process involves making room for all members of the family, including the four-legged ones. There aren't many areas of the house that don't eventually become the pet's domain. Their beds, nests, cushions, and throws can be found in many locations, some of which were never intended for their use. Initially you may feel as though you're ceding space, but when you look into their sweet, wise eyes, you realize you are indeed sharing a space—and a life—with a wet nose that loves you. ●

SLIM AND TRIM

If possible, all pet grooming supplies should be stored in the same space. This pegboard system conveniently holds everything inside a cabinet—from clippers to combs.

FEEDING STATION

This pullout cabinet exactly fits a covered container of dry food. This makes pet feeding easy for you, and predictable for your very hungry pet.

9

ALL HUNG UP

In the smallest of kids' rooms, making use of the bed for storage expands the space. This closet is actually part of a bunk bed system.

toy box, how about buying some open mesh baskets for toy storage? Install a basketball hoop over the open hamper, and just maybe towels or pajamas will end up where they should. Smaller mesh baskets, arranged on shelves, are perfect for doll clothes and make it possible to keep track of those minuscule Barbie sandals and accessories.

If you find clothes balled up under the bed, organize that space with pullout storage for sweaters, sweatshirts, and other bulky items. Turn an old trunk into a home for shoes, sneakers, and boots—call it boot camp and tell the little darlings to "line 'em up!" For their bed, install a bookcase headboard and create a gallery display with some of those old dolls, earless rabbits, and school projects.

Interestingly, some studies have shown that children and adolescents simply seem incapable of hanging clothes on hangers or replacing towels on racks, until they go off to college. Yet they *will* make use of shelves and hooks. That may sound far-fetched, but installing a wall of shelves in the closet, along with the generous use of hooks and pegs on bathroom walls, closet walls, and maybe even in the bedroom, could be the perfect solution to all the disorder. With that many places to actually put things away, you just might catch sight of the floor again! ●

Kid Smarts

YOU CAN'T BELIEVE YOU'RE FAST BECOMING your own mother. When was the last time you heard yourself say: *How many times have I told you to clean your room? Don't leave that wet towel on the floor!* Do these words sound familiar? And you thought that would never happen!

Kids are kids, and mothers are mothers, and despite the cajoling and threats—*Definitely no dessert for you tonight, Young Man!*—it doesn't seem to matter. Children keep on with whatever they were doing, leaving their rooms or closets piled high with clothes, sneakers, games, and toys.

The trouble is children do have a lot of things, and neatness is not a trait most, if any, kids are born with; it must be learned. So instead of yelling and criticizing, help them become better organizers. Instead of that cute little

ONE TO DRAW ON

Even the smallest of tots have stuff to store. This colorful sliding drawer system can graduate from diapers and onesies, to underpants and T-shirts in a few years.

Measuring Up
Cleaning & Storing Dimension Guide

How much space do you really need to Right-Size your laundry, which is your main cleaning area? Each drawing below shows a different possible location for a laundry. Use the recommended (REC), or at least the minimum (MIN) space, needed to make the best use of the space you have.

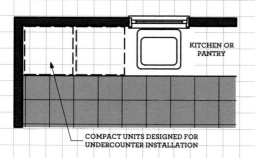

KITCHEN OR PANTRY

COMPACT UNITS DESIGNED FOR UNDERCOUNTER INSTALLATION

LAUNDRY IN KITCHEN

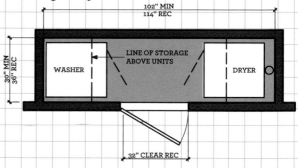

102" MIN
114" REC

30" MIN
36" REC

LINE OF STORAGE ABOVE UNITS

WASHER

DRYER

32" CLEAR REC

LAUNDRY IN CLOSET (FACING EACH OTHER)

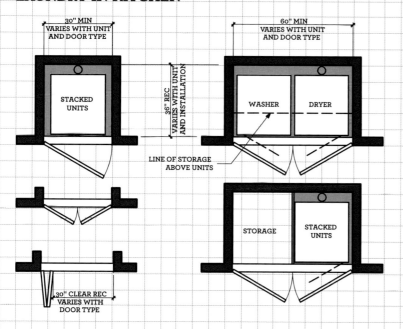

30" MIN
VARIES WITH UNIT AND DOOR TYPE

STACKED UNITS

36" REC VARIES WITH UNIT AND INSTALLATION

60" MIN
VARIES WITH UNIT AND DOOR TYPE

WASHER | DRYER

LINE OF STORAGE ABOVE UNITS

STORAGE | STACKED UNITS

30" CLEAR REC VARIES WITH DOOR TYPE

LAUNDRY IN SMALL CLOSET

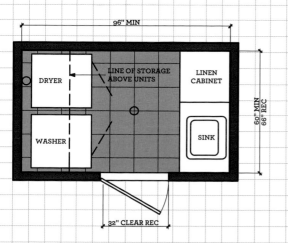

96" MIN

DRYER

LINE OF STORAGE ABOVE UNITS

LINEN CABINET

60" MIN
66" REC

WASHER

SINK

32" CLEAR REC

SMALL LAUNDRY ROOM

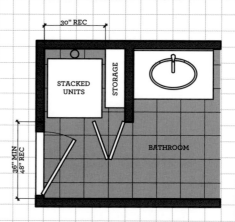

30" REC

STACKED UNITS

STORAGE

36" MIN
48" REC

BATHROOM

LAUNDRY IN BATHROOM

CABINET ORDER

Make smart use of space under the stairs to build in stepped cabinets. They can hide most bulk supplies from the big box stores. No one will ever be the wiser!

Stow Awayer

Hide and Seek

RE YOU THE KIND OF person who carries excess baggage with you no matter where you go? We're talking extra suitcases on the plane here, not the other kind of baggage. You know you need to be equipped for all occasions. In your own home, closets are probably bursting at the seams, and there's no hiding space that's not stuffed to the brim. The need to be prepared for whatever comes your way is both a charm and a curse. You are definitely a Stow Awayer.

Now there is nothing wrong with being the king or queen of storage, if you don't take it too far. Can you really find that great brown T-shirt at a moment's notice? Or where you stowed that silver picture frame you were planning to give your cousin Richie? Yes, the seldom-used fish poacher was only temporarily banished, but can you remember where it is right now? When your lust for even more possessions becomes a liability, it's time to Right-Size.

One of the contributing factors to being a Stow Awayer is those big box stores, where you can buy as though you are feeding a village, even though your children have flown the nest; or you can purchase enough paper supplies to keep every bathroom and kitchen on your street well stocked for the next 16 years! Just because it's a good deal, doesn't mean you have to take it home. Remember to ask yourself: *Where am I going to put this?* The answer can't be, *Somewhere!*

Making sense of what you already own is the first step. Admit that you're really a squirrel with good intentions. The second step is the really hard one. Own up to all the stuff you really have, not just what you think you do. Creating an inventory, closet by closet, will help you get reacquainted with your belongings. Pull absolutely everything out of your cabinets and closets, and you'll be amazed to see what you've really been storing, as well as many things long-lost to the sands of time. Sort your cache into three groups: must-save, *What was I thinking when I bought that?*, and right-into-the-thrift-store bag.

OPEN AND SHUT CASE

This New Age broom closet easily glides out from a dead space near the fridge. The handy bucket on the base level holds smaller sprays and cleaners.

NEAT AND TIDY

There can never be enough hampers in a house to hold all the dirty clothes. These slide-out bins keeps the soiled garments from landing on the floor, and out of sight.

This approach to organization will show you that you really don't have to get rid of everything, and you won't need to cram what you *do* keep back into the closet. (For more help, see "How To Right-Size," Step #3, page 28.)

Once this big sort has been accomplished, move on to the next trouble spot. Eventually, you'll feel lighter, and your possessions may even have some breathing room. Take advantage of this lighthearted moment, and vow to keep your home this orderly. There are a myriad of great products to help you maintain your newly organized areas—from the kitchen, to the bath, to the bedroom, and beyond.

It's a giant step forward to get clothes, accessories, cleaning supplies, and more into uncluttered, accessible places. And you may even find room for new purchases. Oops! What am I saying? ●

Ardent Collector

Collection Agent

OU STARTED WITH one lovely piece, and in a flash, two turned into twenty or more. You can't quite remember precisely when it happened, but that moment defined you as an Ardent Collector. It almost doesn't even matter what you collect, the pieces need room, and you need to find just the right space to house them, store them, or display them—or maybe even drink them.

This is sort of like falling in love. First is the attraction, and then there is lust—your covetous craving for more pieces to add to your grouping, and we're not even calling it a collection yet. Then love takes you to the dark side, and you suddenly end up with multiples of your desire. The question is can you integrate all of these objects of affection into your home? Maybe two or three can be easily displayed, but when the grouping truly becomes a collection, then it's time to assess things before they get seriously out of hand.

I have a friend who loves shoes, and has been instructed by her husband that whenever she brings in a new pair, she must discard an existing pair. What

LIQUID ASSETS

Transform part of a basement into a wine pantry with these professionally designed units. Store wine as well as the necessary glassware and accessories.

does she do? She sends them to her office, and takes them home one shoe at a time. She has shoes hidden under her bed, in the back of her linen closet, and in formerly empty drawers in the guest room. Finally, her desperate spouse called in a professional organizer to help his wife—and her shoes—control themselves! This is an example of an extreme collector, which you, of course, are not.

But how do you, the merely ardent, control yourself and your collection? Start by determining the storage requirements involved, and then move on to consider display needs, if any. What kind of room do you imagine you will need to create a safe haven for this accumulation? Does it need temperature control and special containers? Do you have, or can you acquire, a dust-free cabinet (because you certainly don't want to add to your cleaning duties)? Do you want to show off some or all of the collection? Are there fragile pieces that should be kept out of harm's way? Must the collection be stored/displayed together, or can the pieces be separated? Are you planning to use some of these in your everyday life?

Only you can answer these questions, but keeping them in mind as you add to your collection will be a good reality check.

Remember—there is a very nice lady out there looking for more room for her shoes! ●

THE LITTLE CHILL

Stack wine refrigerators to create individual coolers for both white and red wines, which need slightly different holding temperatures.

FULL OF CHEER

These pullout shelves store non-refrigerated wine bottles at a proper incline, keeping the corks moist.

Space Smarts

NO MATTER WHAT SIZE THE SPACE YOU'VE reserved for cleaning, there should be a sink nearby. Whether you're rinsing out soiled placemats, washing the dog, or repotting some plants, you'll need a source of water for most cleaning activities. Having a place to temporarily make a mess is extremely helpful.

Of course, your kitchen sink is probably the place of first resort for many cleaning actions, because it's in such a frequently used location. The laundry room, if you have a separate space for this, usually has a larger or deeper sink, which works well for all-purpose tasks.

Today's new family entry, the mudroom, sometimes has an auxiliary sink to help keep the outside dirt from making its way inside. It's an easy way to handle muddy dog paws, or clean a "boo-boo" on a child's skinned knee. Use it to wash off muddy gardening gloves, golf shoe cleats, or hands messy from the afternoon cookout.

Sinks are a homeowner's best friend these days, and the cleaning process may include soaking, washing, rinsing, or any combination of the three. Think creatively about the size of the basin. If space permits, select one that is either wider or deeper than you think you need. Deeper sinks don't take any more horizontal space than shallow versions, but you will have to trade

AWASH WITH STYLE

An extra sink is always a good thing. This one goes from being a potting center to rinsing bathing suits, and gives meaning to the phrase "utility sink."

SOAK IT TO ME

You're ready for almost anything with a deep, stainless steel sink.

off space if you select a wider variety. The benefits might well outweigh the loss of counter area.

The old-fashioned laundry sink, with a drain board attached, can still be used for a myriad of household tasks, such as washing a small dog. Keep surplus towels stacked on the drain board. Similarly, a wide, double bowl sink can masquerade as a cooler for beverages at parties, or as a site for cutting and arranging flowers (never a neat job). It's also a great place to rinse freshly harvested vegetables from the garden or for the final cleaning of the rewards from that fishing trip.

A personal favorite is the multifunctional, extra-deep, stainless steel sink—typically a laundry sink—frequently used for dishwashing at commercial restaurants. However, in the family kitchen it can hide a multitude of sins when covered over with a cutting board, such as concealing a growing mound of pots and pans during a holiday feast. It's also handy as an emergency place to stash the dirty dishes when unexpected company comes—you get the picture! ●

Now It's Your Turn

Right-Sizing *Your* Storing Area

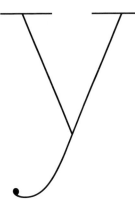

YOU MAY NEED TO REASSESS YOUR STORING SPACES, because they no longer work for your needs. You could add a few more things to the duty roster of the mudroom, like recharging cell phones or iPods there. Try rearranging the laundry room to fit those two recycling bins you've had your eye on. And cleaning supplies do need to be stored near the user. Refer to the "Style Audit," "Redesign Plan," and "Dimension Guide" to help you rethink your space and storing style, no matter what you squirrel away. ●

Specific Storage Spaces versus Multifunctional Spaces

THINK DEDICATED DROP ZONE	RETHINK MULTIFUNCTIONAL	THINK DEDICATED SUPPLY CABINET
Designate a portion of the mudroom specifically for household key storage, as well as for leaving messages. A shelf with labeled key hooks and chargers right near the door is handy. This will help everyone make use of the convenience as they enter the house.	*Make an already hardworking room, such as a laundry or kitchen, act as a recycling center. A clever use of cabinets can keep cans, bottles, newspapers, and cardboard separate and contained.*	*Instead of having soaps and cleaners stored randomly around the house, use a handy, under-cabinet, pullout caddy to keep them together in one central location, saving you time and energy.*
RESULTS: *Allows more flexible space*	**RESULTS:** *More features in same space*	**RESULTS:** *More space created*

Live Fully

There is no end to the Right-Sizing process. The idea is to keep up by paring down. Once you've actually tackled clearing out the clutter, you can begin to think about what you really want. What you need today will surely change as tomorrow rolls around. Living fully means living in comfort, and by Right-Sizing, you and your family will indeed live in comfort throughout your home—now and in the years ahead.

How To Start Paring Down

Think of paring down as putting your house on a diet. *When it's the recipient of too much accumulated stuff and starts bulging at the seams, like a pair of pants getting too tight, then it's time to take control of the clutter.*

A FRIEND FROM BOSTON, Standolyn Robertson—a Certified Professional Organizer (CPO), whose business is helping people de-clutter their lives and homes—hosts a website (www.thingsinplace.com) that is filled with the most helpful hints. Her three-statement test (box below) can help you determine just how badly you need to get your house back in shape.

> ## "You know you are ready for a change, when:
>
> o *Clutter at home interferes with your ability to meet personal and family demands, and these same demands keep you from getting organized*
> o *Valuable items or papers get lost, mislaid bills go unpaid—and it's costing you*
> o *You don't invite guests to your home because you're embarrassed, or because there's no room for them"*

Now you may not be in such dire straits as these. Perhaps only a few areas of the house have gotten out of control. If you've been working at paring down, you've been lucky to contain the mess in at least one room. But who's kidding whom? Somehow more stuff will come through the door, whether you bring it home or not.

Maybe you'll inherit possessions from your parents or a close relative. This can be dangerous because there's a sentimental attachment involved, and you'll most likely find yourself becoming the caretaker of these belongings. It's easy to find your home overtaken by furniture and accessories that have no place in your life. Try to sort through things before you bring them home, and have a good friend at your side, ready to be an objective eye.

A second source of clutter is children's ephemera. Like magnets, they acquire toys, games, and other things as they grow up, yet they never get rid of the bulk of them. Eventually your children leave home, but you continue to manage a warehouse for all those childhood belongings. Try to get the kids to finally claim what they've left behind.

Your own shopping habits are a third source. You spot something on sale and rush off to reap the reward of a new lamp or chair. The problem is what are you going to do with the items that you're replacing? Suddenly filled with remorse, you can't bring yourself to throw away the originals, and now you have two of them. So you move the older piece to another room, and...ooops! Guess what? You missed a golden moment to recycle the older item out the door.

Gifts, large and small, can actually add to the house's clutter. Even if unwanted, they can become permanent residents. Please be careful. If you can't use the present, no matter how well intentioned, then don't let it add to the clutter confusion. Plan to return it to the store, if feasible. Otherwise, quietly recycle it to someone else who might make good use of it, or donate it to your favorite charity. Whatever you do, do not keep what you do not want or cannot use. This is a good habit to keep.

Another source of continually ever-mounting stuff is family office work or schoolwork, and when paired with what the mailman brings, there can be an ongoing battle of paper. Newspapers, magazines, books, notepapers, flyers, mail, and catalogs are all guilty denizens when left alone, unattended in your house. They wind up in piles, refusing to vacate the premises.

Even if this is just a vague description of your own

collection of clutter, then you know what I mean. Before you can do some serious Right-Sizing, you need to weed out the excess, and cull through your belongings until you have what you actually need and will truly use. As you sort, plan for your future needs as well, if at all possible.

If you can't take on this chore, then it may be time to invest in the services of a professional organizer (see "Resources," page 200). He or she can help you set realistic goals, assess your belongings in the context of these goals, and then assist you in organizing your room or rooms. This is how you begin to Right-Size, and see what space you really have, instead of guessing at the space hiding under mounds of possessions.

The information below and over the next few pages is aimed at helping you prepare for the changes you'll make—and appreciate—as you Right-Size your home.

How To Get Rid Of The Clutter

Part of Right-Sizing is starting with an almost clean slate in the room that you're *working on. That means getting rid of the stuff you've accumulated over time that doesn't belong there. Okay, some of those papers have almost become part of the family by now!*

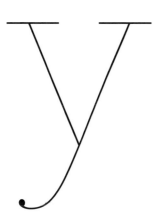

YOU KNOW ABOUT THE "One-Two-Three Method" that was described in Step #3, "Getting Rid of What You Don't Want," on page 28. Use "yes," "no," and "maybe"—words to identify piles of items you are either going to keep, discard, or think about.

The objective is to divide those extra belongings into two piles, then after a trip to your favorite charity, only one remains, which gets put away or filed.

Let's take a closer look at the "yes" pile. You may want to store some of the items with similar things in another room, rather than the room you're currently Right-Sizing. So, divide the "yes" pile into two: "stay here" or "stay elsewhere" categories.

There is one big question to ask yourself: *How often do I use this?* There are only three possible answers: frequently, infrequently, or very infrequently.

How often do I use these items?

o *Frequently (meaning daily or weekly)*
o *Infrequently (less than weekly, but ongoing)*
o *Very Infrequently (once or twice a year, or for special entertaining)*

If an item is in the "frequently" category, it deserves to stay right there where you need it. An extra throw for the sofa, or toilet paper supply is in this group. For something in the "infrequently" section, place it where you can find it again. It doesn't have to stay in the room. Think about paper shredders or large platters here. Finally, if "very infrequently," it definitely does not belong in the room, but in a *clearly marked storage area* so you don't have to hunt for it again. Chafing dishes or fish poachers belong here.

That was simple, wasn't it? You are sorted, cleared, and cleaned out. Maybe you feel so good about it, you want to start on the next room? Or, perhaps it's time to take a break and have a piece of chocolate as a reward for a job well done.

10

Right-Sizing Action Plan

WHETHER YOU'RE GETTING READY TO REORGANIZE, remodel, or maybe even move, there are certain steps necessary to make the Right-Sizing process move ahead smoothly. The disruption of routine is going to be stressful on you and your family. There will be uncertainty, upset schedules, and unforeseen delays. To help yourself and everyone else, follow the steps below to make these changes as least disturbing as possible. Also, don't forget to review specific chapters for helpful checklists that pertain to a particular room or activity.

Be Realistic

Be clear about your expectations. Learn when to draw the line between what's desirable and what's essential. Any change, even clearing out your belongings, will alter the appearance of your home, and most renovations will add to the equity in your home. If you are planning to stay in your present location, think of the improved comfort, added convenience, easier maintenance, or the simple pleasure of a fresh new look.

On the other hand, you can overdo a good thing. If you plan to move within a few years, is the renovation really worth it? Does it pay to add an expensive new addition when your house is in an area of more modest homes? Will you get the return on your investment?

Create a Budget

Determine how much you can comfortably spend on this project, then add another 25 to 30 percent for emergencies or changes. Nothing ever goes smoothly. In your financial plan, you need to allow for unforeseen obstacles, such as delays or other complications. This will help you keep both your dollars, and schedule, under control. Multiple estimates will give you a good idea of what to expect.

Arrange for financing after you have an acceptable bid from a contractor, and investigate a range of funding options. Home improvement financing means the lender will secure your financing using the equity value of your house. Decide whether you want a home equity credit line, or a home improvement, fixed-rate loan.

Design a Plan

Once you have decided what types of changes you want, get all your ideas down on paper. Make a floor plan, measuring all the fixed items in your space. Pull out all those clippings of ideas you've been saving, to help clearly explain the parameters of your goals to your contractor, or other design professional.

You should consider the worthwhile investment in the skills and knowledge of an architect, designer, or professional organizer to finalize the plan. You will get back what you pay out by having a better design. While you might try out home renovation software on your computer, plan to use that only as a starting point for the project.

Create a Timetable

Using your plan as a guide, devise a timeline that you and your contractor or design professionals can follow. Understand that Murphy's Law will apply no matter how organized you think you are, and that the timetable will change. This is real life, not a television show!

A good hint is to try to stockpile what will be needed ahead of schedule. Ask your contractor to order items far enough in advance, so they will be available by the time they are needed for the project. This means, of course, you will have to pre-shop for all parts of the project, so your own choices don't hold up the progress. Allow yourself adequate time to do this in the beginning of the project, and you will reap the reward of avoiding delays near the end.

Attend to Legal Issues

You must have a written contract with your builder, not just a written quote. The contractor will organize agreements with the subcontractors. However, if you are managing the project yourself, under a labor-only contract with the builder, you will have to arrange binding agreements with each of the contractors (the plasterers, painters, and plumbers, for example). When all the terms and conditions are clearly spelled out and recorded in writing, it means there is less room for argument about who is responsible if something goes wrong.

Have all necessary permit applications filed, and permits issued in advance of project commencement. If you are doing a major renovation, you need to be aware of potential building code issues. Discuss potential problems in advance with building inspectors.

6 Hold a Family Conference

Sit down with everyone in your family to talk about the Right-Sizing project timeline, and how it will impact their daily activities. Anticipate their fears. Discuss how newly designated areas and limited resources (e.g., bathrooms) are to be used. Use a little humor and imagination to keep everyone anticipating the end goal. If there's going to be a delay or a change in the project, tell everyone in the family as far in advance as possible.

Surprise meals or little celebrations help the family remain flexible and better able to endure the temporary hardships that are guaranteed to occur during a Right-Sizing process. These include living through the constant noise of banging, hammering, sawing or drilling, the endless production of dust, or a sea of boxes.

7 Keep a Record

Before you begin any actual construction, take photos of the existing space—even the inside and outside of closets or cabinets. These will be your "before" images, and provide a good way to remind you how much stuff you had. As you sort through your possessions, make a list of items you no longer use, to help you eliminate unnecessary things. Periodically take "during" photos to track improvements. Finish up the project with "after" shots. This photographic inventory will serve as a record of the creation of your new space. You might even assemble the pictures into a "new room" album to share with friends or keep for future reference.

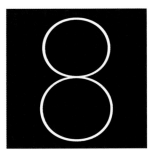

8 Itemize What You Need

This is another sort of record keeping. As you embark on Right-Sizing, grab a notebook and create a master list, with all the things you will need to successfully complete the project. Which possessions can be moved within your home for safekeeping, and which need to be stored elsewhere? Identify items that need a new home, and offer them to family members or friends who might use them.

If you're moving or temporarily storing during a remodel, this list may include packing boxes, bubble wrap, heavy-duty tape, permanent markers, and stick-on labels to identify contents. If you're weeding out, use some of the same supplies for transporting unwanted goods to thrift shops, resale stores, garage sales, or even to ship things after your successful online auction.

Obtain Temporary Storage

Leasing temporary storage space is an alternative you should consider when embarking on major projects, whether you are renovating or preparing for a move. Resist the temptation to pile everything into your garage or basement. You want to protect your valuables from breakage or moisture damage, and gain more room in the process.

Choose a space that best fits your needs on a temporary basis. You may opt to move your belongings to an easy-access, independent self storage unit, or even a pod storage unit that can be located in your yard. Depending on where you live, climate controlled storage may be necessary. Ask about the use of dollies or heavy-duty carts, so you can easily move your goods in and out.

Soothe Pets and Children

Last, but certainly not least, are the smaller members of the family. Their daily routine will be changed for weeks or even months to come. It may be necessary to move out of the house, however temporarily, which will further dislocate everyone.

If possible, select an area of your home—one that will not be affected by the construction—to become the new "family room" for eating, watching TV, doing homework, playing games, etc.

The more difficult challenge is how to not upset the pets, who are creatures of habit. Bringing their bedding, blankets, water and food bowls, or familiar toys to the family room will help ease their transition as well.

Don't turn the page without reading this last paragraph!

Now that you understand the Right-Sizing process, and have all the tools you need to begin rethinking and reinventing the space you have, there is one more thing you need to consider. Many of us focus on how comfortable we are in our homes at the moment. But true Right-Sizing also requires us to pay attention to our comfort needs as we age. The next chapter reveals small modifications that can be hidden in plain sight, but will allow you and your family to be comfortable in your new space—not just in the present, but as you face your future. Now, turn the page.

Where You Live In Comfort

The Sesame Street song, "One of These Things (Is Not Like the Others)," *reminds me that we are all different from one another, and therefore, deserve special attention when it comes to living fully, safely, and with ease in our homes.*

OME OF US ARE HEIGHT-CHALLENGED. WE ARE either too short (maybe not tall enough, you feel?) or too tall, peering down at people's heads. In either case, many activities in the home require working at uncomfortable levels or reaching to awkward heights. Do you have to stretch to grasp something in those upper cabinets, without using a stepladder? Is the normal countertop height too low or too high? Are you forced to double over the sink to wash your hands and face? Forget about actually getting on your knees to find something located in the back of the sink cabinet! (See the "Comfort Dimension Guide," page 195, for reach range specifics.)

Many older adults prefer to live independently, but find themselves moving about more slowly and wobbly. Simple things that used to be done around the house (without thinking) are now a source of fear. Even the pleasures of getting in and out of the bathtub, or simply pulling hot food out of the oven can be a trial.

Still others have serious, long-term impairments that make maneuvering around the house extremely arduous. The sad news is that despite the Americans with Disabilities Act, most homes are not designed with access for the disabled in mind. The bathroom doorway is too narrow, or countertops are too high. Even moving across different floor surfaces—from carpet to rugs to hardwood—make the passage from room to room a journey in itself.

Then there are those of us who seem to have the word "accident" written all over us. Clumsily slipping on stairs, banging into table corners or dishwasher edges, or slicing and dicing our fingers are good examples of mishaps we've endured. Distracted by the phone and running to answer it, we didn't see the uneven rug that tripped us and landed us smack on the floor. The list could go on and on, and individuals can be any age.

The truth is our homes can be a hazard to us all, and living in comfort without fear is key. Time to reexamine your rooms, and the traffic flow among them. Time to create small, simple Right-Sizing changes to make moving, working, and relaxing around the home work best for everyone, from small to tall, to uncertain, to seated, to awkward. That's universal design.

CLEAR THE WAY

You would never guess that this handsome hallway is a good example of universal design. The generous width, lack of scatter rug, and non-skid flooring make the room inviting to all who enter.

What is Universal Design?

A well-planned home should be totally user-friendly, no matter who uses it.
That is what universal design is all about. In the hardest working rooms of the house—
the kitchen, laundry, and bathrooms—this is particularly true, and being efficient in
your use of space makes those rooms more enjoyable to live and work in.

FITTED FOR PURPOSE

*Working at the right height is important
for your long-term comfort. Elevate built-in
appliances so you can easily reach their
contents. The ideal height for your wall
oven or microwave is waist high. The
dishwasher can be raised eight inches, for
better access without stressing your back.*

MADE TO MEASURE

*The right amount of workspace is directly
related to the number of paces you take
to go from one appliance to another. Too
much countertop area will mean you have
further to walk or walk around. Storage
space needs to be planned the same way, so
that you don't waste space, or walk too far.*

HOT TOPIC

*It may make sense to consider lowering
your cooktop a few inches, if you
haven't placed your oven beneath it.
This allows you to peer inside larger
pots, and particularly if you're short,
having that lowered will help you
avoid straining while cooking.*

Comfort Style Audit

*Select the comfort style that best describes you.
Then follow the tips below
to help you be safe and sound in your home.*

ARE YOU A LEISURELY PACER?

○ Can't admit your vision/hearing isn't what it used to be
○ Tend to take your physical skills for granted
○ Value your independence; have a hard time asking for help

TIPS:

- Have your house evaluated by a Certified Aging-in-Place Specialist (CAPS) for simple changes (see "Resources," page 200)
- Arrange kitchen cabinets for easy access to heavy items; install wall cabinets that move up and down for easy reach

- Use a front-loading laundry machine raised 12 to 15 inches from the floor, side by side or bottom-mount refrigerator-freezers, and induction cooktops
- Avoid knobs on doors, cabinets, appliances, or faucets; install levers to push; use electronic or touch controls on appliances

ARE YOU A SMALL PERSON?

○ Your best friend in your home is the step stool
○ Secretly move your possessions to the lower drawers
○ Like sitting on a barstool because you feel taller

TIPS:

- Keep your frequently used items in plain sight; apply to kitchen items, china, glassware, clothes, shoes, etc.
- Hang everyday clothes on lower rods; use pull-down versions as upper rods; fold more clothes to store on shelves or in drawers

- Use easy open/shut drawer-style appliances; they now include microwaves, dishwashers, refrigerators, and freezers
- Adjust height of bathroom mirror; one that tilts can increase visibility, and be repositioned for each user

ARE YOU ACCIDENTALLY INCLINED?

○ Sharp corners of tables/counters attract you like a magnet
○ Always have adhesive/elastic bandages and slings at hand
○ Easily distracted by phone, TV, music; have trouble focusing

TIPS:

- Concentrate on kitchen/bathroom activities; never run for phone or door; secure area rugs throughout house
- Eliminate shadow or glare with good lighting; install nightlights or sensor lights to avoid stumbling in the middle of the night

- Choose kitchen or bath countertops with rounded edges; use child-safe corner guards on low tables or ones you frequently encounter
- Use silicon pot holders for all hot pots or pans; replace batteries for carbon monoxide and fire alarms

ARE YOU LONG LEGGED?

○ You look down to make conversation with most people
○ The top shelf is always easiest for you to reach
○ You bump your head on the tops of doorframes

TIPS:

- Replace your showerhead with an adjustable or hand-held model
- Raise built-in appliances further off the floor if possible; a wall oven can be placed as high as 40 inches; raise your dishwasher 12 inches

- If sharing a kitchen, create a separate work surface for yourself at 42 inches high; other counters can remain at 36 inches
- If sharing a bathroom, a detached sink and countertop will allow you to use a higher level than your partner

ARE YOU WELL SEATED?

○ Spend most of your time in a seated position
○ Have limited access to items above your head
○ Find it hard navigating your home without assistance

TIPS:

- Plan a 60-inch turning radius in bathroom; install grab bars; use a curbless shower at least 36 inches wide; raise toilet to comfort height of 17 to 19 inches
- Rethink counter spaces to make room for dishes or clothes adjacent/opposite appliances; for safety, use cooktop with level burners

- Ensure a minimum 36-inch width in passageways, halls, and rooms; invest in skid-proof flooring
- Place light switches, thermostats, and other controls no higher than 40 inches from the floor; make sure rocker or touch switches are installed at each entryway

Small Person
Just My Size

SHRINK FIT

Consider creating a lower-height island that provides a comfortable work surface. You can later add casters to raise the height, if needed.

EOPLE LOOK UP TO those who are tall, but if you are short, life is a bit more difficult. You're always trying to measure up—or even catch up, if your activities involve walking or running. You have great empathy for those who are even closer to the ground...like dachshunds. When you're a diminutive person, you take a movie title such as *Get Shorty,* very personally.

In fact, the struggle continues in your home. To be able to reach your possessions is a sort of daily confrontation with cabinets, closets, and countertops, none of which were designed with you in mind.

Just starting the day is a chore if you haven't Right-Sized your bathroom. Getting to your things can be a reach if they're not under the counter. You've probably learned to cope, however, and tend to leave your clutter on the countertop as a result. Instead, invest in some of those ingenious cabinet inserts, which let you organize your makeup and other necessities inside the cabinets. Medicine cabinets have also been reinvented, and you no longer require extension grabbers to retrieve those vitamins that migrated to an upper shelf. Also, instead of struggling to reach over the sink, look for

SMALL BUT MIGHTY

Small, built-in steam ovens can be a cook's friend, but when placed at waist height, they're easier for a shorter cook, too.

ANOTHER LEVEL

If reaching up is a struggle, think about a hydraulic wall cabinet that lowers to your own reach.

longer, thinner cabinets that wall mount or recess, and can be placed at a height convenient for you.

Your closet is another minefield, because getting at your clothes and shoes frequently requires daily use of a step stool. Lowering the closet rod to a comfortable height may mean compromising hanging versus folding space, but getting at your favorite clothes is easily the best reward.

Anything at countertop height is accessible, but some of your wall cabinets are probably off-limits without help, or that step stool again. To judge how high the wall cabinets should be positioned, measure the height you can safely reach (no tippy toes please!). That should be the *maximum* shelf distance for your most frequently used china, glassware, or food supplies. Generally, lowering your upper cabinets three inches gives you a 15-inch backsplash instead of the usual 18-inch one, but will give you more easy-to-reach storage.

Appliances can also test you as a small person. Built-in microwaves, and other ovens, should be lowered to 36 inches from the floor. If you are the primary cook, you might consider lowering your cooktop as well.

Remember, in any reorganization of either the kitchen or bath, you have "first dibs" on the lower shelves or base cabinets. ●

Comfort Redesign Plan

Before implementing universal design changes to your kitchen, bath, and/or laundry, look at the lists below. The items you check should help guide you in assessing your space, and how it might work best for you. Use these responses to define the problems, as well as the solutions.

Reasons for making a change?

(check all that apply)

O Room does not fit needs

O Closet inadequate for specific users

O Need accessible tub or shower

O Poor cabinet storage accessories

O Better storage management

O No lever hardware

O Poorly located light switches and outlets

O Doors and passageway are too narrow

O Flooring not slip-resistant

O Faucet and showerhead need replacing

O Space to sort or fold clothes

O Appliances not easy to use

O No room for maneuvering

Who uses this room?

(check all that apply)

O Adults

O Older adults

O Children

O Guests

O Pets

How is it used?

(check all that apply)

O Bathing

O Sleeping

O Clothes/shoes storage

O Cooking

O Relaxing

O Working

O Cleaning

O Eating

What do you need to store here?

(check all that apply)

O Food

O China and glassware

O Cookware

O Personal beauty items

O Medicine and medical supplies

O Pet supplies

O Laundry supplies

O Cleaning supplies

O Clothes

O Coats and outerwear

O Books, CDs, DVDs, games

O Personal or work files

What do you need for more comfort?

(check all that apply)

O Personalized closet space

O Easy-access storage space

O Multilevel workspaces/countertops

O Better cabinet organization

O Accessible appliance placement

O Pull-down shelves or cabinetry

O Appropriate grab bars and supports

O Individual shower/tub needs

O Lever hardware for doors, cabinets, faucet, or shower

O Slip-resistant flooring surfaces

Trade-Offs

As you map out a plan to Right-Size for comfort and efficiency, think about the trade-offs below. Remember to take into consideration the amount of space you really have, while weighing wants versus needs.

	VERSUS			VERSUS	
Base Cabinets w/Drawers	◄►	**Base Cabinets w/Doors**	**Lever Handle Faucet**	◄►	**Knob Handle Faucets**
Easy access; clear sight lines		Difficult; obstructed view	Easy to operate		Requires firmer grip
Lowered Microwave	◄►	**Microwave Above Oven**	**Comfort Height Toilet**	◄►	**Low Seat Toilet**
Easy to reach		Stretch to reach	Easy to sit and stand		Difficult to sit and stand
Raised Dishwasher	◄►	**Floor-mounted Dishwasher**	**Hand-Held Shower**	◄►	**Wall-Mounted Shower**
Easy to load and unload		Requires more bending	Easy to handle		Limited adjustment
Front-Load Washer/Dryer	◄►	**Top-Load Washer/Dryer**	**Walk-In Tub**	◄►	**Standard Step-Over Tub**
Easy to view contents		Need to be standing	Easy, safe entry		Hazardous without grab bars

You can appreciate the flexible height of these wall cabinets, when they've been raised for your convenience.

Long Legged
On The Rise

IFE IS DIFFERENT WHEN YOU ARE particularly tall. You stand out in a crowd, for example. People make assumptions about your basketball skills, not realizing that you couldn't possibly hit the side of a barn, even if you wanted to! It's not easy living up to those elevated expectations.

What makes being very tall even more of a challenge is that most homes—whether house, condo, or apartment—are not designed for anyone over six feet tall. Sure you can reach the top shelf in the kitchen with ease, but how about those bottom drawers or lowest shelves? You'd have to be a contortionist to get at the things so inconveniently stored. *Why don't they make drawers that rise up?* you wonder. How about elevating the dishwasher? And while the kitchen designers are at it, the sinks don't have to be so low, do they?

Of course, if you live with someone who is shorter than yourself, you hear the argument that he or she needs full access to the kitchen, and there are standard measurements for cabinets. Your aching back doesn't agree. But when your spouse or partner finally agrees to elevate one counter from the customary 36 inches, to a comfortable 42 inches, you'll be feeling a whole lot better.

Moving onto the bathroom—another area of heated, lower-level discussion. You certainly would like to do your ablutions at a better height. If your bathroom hasn't been renovated recently, you might still be bending over an old 27-inch high vanity. The newer, adult-height vanities have risen to the standard 36 inches, which is a modest improvement. Unfortunately, it's difficult to find 42-inch versions, in which case you might opt for a wall-mounted unit.

You've compromised in the shower with a hand-held showerhead, rather than forcing yourself to crouch beneath that poorly positioned, wall-mounted model. You also won the battle over replacing the standard, low-to-the-ground toilet (14 to 15 inches) with one that is at a "comfort height" (16½ to 17 inches), and everyone who uses the bathroom now agrees it's an improvement.

At least your workspace at home actually fits your stature. Home office designers understand the needs of the tall. Your desk chair not only adjusts to your height, but it has an innovative neck support that feels ever so good. You planned your work surface to meet your loftier needs.

Even though *Sesame Street*'s Kermit the Frog has been telling us for years that it's not easy being green, you know it's not easy at all to be very tall! ●

IT'S HIGH TIME

New wall cabinets feature a lift-up mechanism that folds the door upward, to permit full access.

RAISING THE BAR

Grab bars on a tub or shower are great for the very tall, whose center of gravity is so high.

Leisurely Pacer

Coming of Age

O ONE EVER WANTS to think of themselves as getting older. This is particularly true if you are a member of the Baby Boom generation. You're certainly not alone. There are some 77.3 million of you, and the leading edge of the group began turning 60 in 2006. While you may not like to face the fact that you're close to retirement, you are definitely not retiring from life.

Unlike your parents, who seemed old at 65, you have no plans to move into a retirement community if you can help it. Most likely, your goal is to stay in your own home and age gracefully.

The unfortunate term for this is "aging-in-place!"

Regardless, the good news is you can start thinking ahead about making modifications to your home that will accommodate age-related changes in your life. Of course, no one wants their beautiful home to be altered to the extent where it looks like a dismal convalescent center, but we can't envision the place as an obstacle course one day either. Luckily, manufacturers are getting your quiet message, and are creating products in good taste and good design, that disguise the ways in which they will help keep you more independent some day.

You might start in the bathroom to assess the alterations needed. Slip-resistant floor tile, for example, can help—not hinder—your movements; that's a simple choice. Great looking grab bars (not the institutional

BEST LAID PLANS

The temptation to tile is strongest in the bathroom. Be sure to select non-slip tiles for all surface applications.

type) can be put in place now, and act as towel bars—until eventually needed for their original purpose. Raise the height of your toilet to a "comfort height" of 16½ to 17 inches, and change the size of the opening of the bath doorway from 30 inches to 36 inches wide. These are discreet adaptations, which mean no one will be the wiser—except you and your contractor.

The kitchen also has potential for adjustments beyond updating its looks. Visual problems are one of the body's physical changes most of us don't anticipate. Appliance controls, and the labels associated with them, should be effortless to read. For example, one new advance is a wall oven that employs larger type and greater contrast to make the words easier to read.

Accessibility to higher-level storage diminishes as time moves on. But base cabinets with rollout trays, lazy Susans, and effortlessly gliding drawers are hidden assets that you can use now in either the kitchen or bathroom—as well as later.

It's never too early to begin thinking about convenient storage for medicines. Another double-benefit, now available, is a wall-mounted bath cabinet with refrigeration on one side to keep perishable drugs longer. Since you probably don't need that feature yet, use it instead for longer-lived cosmetics—to keep yourself looking younger! ●

PERFECT FIT

Bring your heavy cookware to you with an easy-pull cabinet insert, allowing you to access the entire contents.

NECESSARY GOOD

What a clever idea to add a little refrigeration to your medicine cabinet! It keeps fragile drugs and cosmetics fresher, longer.

EASY REACH

Showering in a seated position is safer and more secure. Try a hand-held shower system; it's great for this purpose.

Accidentally Inclined

Protect Yourself

OW MANY TIMES DO people say "Watch out!" or "Watch your step!" to you? Probably more than you would care to admit. When you're not paying attention, or are distracted, safety is something easily ignored. And of course, as one of the myriad of accident-prone people who keep crashing into, slipping, or even cutting or burning themselves, you pay the consequences because you were not totally focused. Safety is a big issue for the Accidentally Inclined.

Every room can be a hazard if you're not careful. Watching where you're going means you need to be on alert for potential hazards. Since sharp corners of tables or countertops, as well as drawers or doors that are not completely closed, are menaces, look for furniture with rounded edges that are more friendly to your hips or arms. Also, especially for the kitchen and bath, there are new, soft-close mechanisms that close bottom drawers, which may save you an unnecessary bruised

GETTING THE HANG OF IT

Instead of struggling to reach your clothes, let something else do the work. This pull-down system makes for a trouble-free retrieval.

WATCH YOUR STEP

If you are always bumping into things, then this easy-close drawer design will help you avoid bruised shins, or worse.

shin. And slip-resistant flooring is a must for your most frequented pathways through the house. Even little details such as non-slip pads under smaller rugs can prevent unneeded falls.

Having trouble dealing with your clothes closet? Try to avoid using a step stool if you can. Bringing your clothes to you instead of going to them is a far better idea. Plan better access to your garments by placing everyday items within a safe and easy reach. Use conveniently placed hooks or shelves for bulkier items. Improve the lighting to help evade your potential for instability. And use a stable chair when putting on socks or hose.

Sensing danger at every turn in your bathroom? Hot water temperature-control valves for both faucets, as well as the showerhead, are a must to avoid scalds or burns. Exchange that fixed showerhead for a hand-held version that can also be attached to a vertical rod and slid up and down for ease of use. Install grab bars by the tub, as well as the shower. Lighting and exhaust fans with motion sensor controls, enhance safety and save energy, too. Similarly, adding Ground Fault Interrupt (GFI) to the electrical outlets in your bathroom is absolutely mandatory. And of course, personal care appliances should be used at a distance from any water sources to avoid getting shocked—or worse.

Expecting a disaster in the kitchen? Well, appliances have gotten smarter, and many make good considerations for the accident-prone. There's an induction cooktop that sounds an alarm if a liquid boils over. Similarly, look for an electric cooktop with a Sensor Dome feature that monitors and adjusts a pot's temperature, keeping it from boiling over.

Whatever investments you make to ensure your home safety, the changes will also benefit all members of the family. Safety isn't only for the Accidentally Inclined—it's for everyone. ●

SECRET AGENT

Children will be a lot safer if they learn to hold on to grab bars when bathing.

happens, are exercises that benefit everyone, no matter what their age.

Falls are a big problem for the young. Wherever water may get splashed around, slip-resistant flooring makes sense for kids of all ages, as well as adults. If you must have scatter or area rugs, be sure to install self-adhesive pads underneath.

Bathrooms are one of the most potentially hazardous areas—there are a litany of dangers you can find online. Think ahead with grab bars that are easy to reach, non-slip surfaces, and plumbing designed with younger people in mind. Non-scalding controls, hand-held showerheads, and automatic on/off valves for faucets are a good start in any bathroom where kids have access.

Remember, whatever you install for your children makes good sense for whomever uses the space, even you. ●

Kid Smarts

ARE CHILDREN REALLY ACCIDENTS WAITING
to happen? The answer is both yes and no, and much depends on the parent or caregiver's philosophy of how kids learn about danger. If you're in the overprotective school of thought, you will probably go into overdrive during the toddler to preteen years, and then hopefully relax. On the other side of the spectrum, you could be a *laissez-faire* parent who says children will learn about safety as they make mistakes. There is a middle ground in this discussion, and that's where most parents find themselves.

Being careful in those early years, with protective guards of all shapes and sizes, was only the beginning of parental guidance. You were, of course, alert to dangers, both real and potential, as you taught your children about slipping and falling, fire and smoke, and other hazards of the house over which you have some—but not total—control. Was this a one-time lesson, or did you repeat it for retention? Family activities, such as a yearly fire drill or discussing whom to contact if something serious

ON GUARD

Keeping ingredients or supplies out of harm's way is easier with this backsplash storage unit, which sits deep on the counter.

Measuring Up

Comfort Dimension Guide

Right-Sizing with universal design in the working areas of your home means accommodating each member of the family, whether tall or short, young or old, flexible or infirm. Refer to the reach ranges and tips below, to provide comfort and usability for everyone.

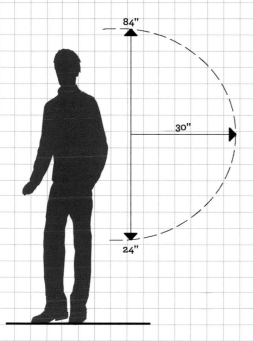

TALL

84"
30"
24"

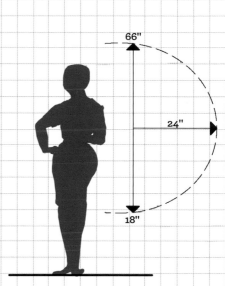

SHORT

66"
24"
18"

GENERAL TIPS:

- Use the reach ranges shown to optimize the locations of clothes rods, shelves, cabinets, etc.
- Full-extension drawers or slide-out trays help avoid reaching deep into cabinets
- Consider a drawer-type dishwasher mounted just below a counter, for easy access
- For greater comfort and access, counters and cooktops can be set higher or lower than the standard 36-inch countertop height
- Extra shelves in cabinets mean reduced stacking, allowing easier access
- Provide specific storage areas for each family member for more convenient access
- Protect small children by investing in locking hardware for lower cabinets
- Be aware of, and anticipate, the changing needs of growing children and aging adults
- Touch-activated faucets, thermostatic shower valves, and lighting controls can make life safer and more comfortable

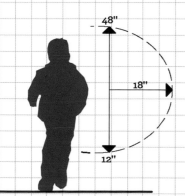

CHILD

48"
18"
12"

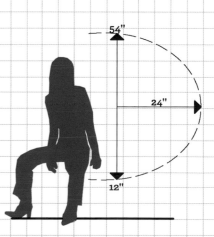

SEATED

54"
24"
12"

Well Seated

The Right Move

LOT OF LIP SERVICE IS given to the idea of accessibility. The Americans with Disabilities Act (ADA) created helpful guidelines, but its code compliance is focused mainly on provisions for those who spend their days confined to a wheelchair. What about those who are not seated, but need equal access to safety and security? What about those whose needs are not permanent, but a temporary setback? When you need a helping hand, your home should accommodate you without a struggle, whether Well Seated or not.

Only you know best how you move around the house. Is it with ease or effort? Are stairs a major problem? Can you use the kitchen independently when you want? Does the bathroom require a great effort to maneuver? Is moving from room to room more of an obstacle course than a smooth ride? Do you use a tremendous amount of physical effort to do chores that are, by nature, simple to handle?

If you answered yes to any of these questions, you are ready for a Right-Sizing that incorporates universal design principles. Ponder the body size, posture, and mobility of all family members as you plan changes. Be sure to refer to the "Comfort Dimension Guide" on page 195 for specific reach ranges.

For ease of movement, ensure a minimum 36-inch width in hallways and rooms; for doorways, allow 32 inches

of clear space with flush, or minimal, thresholds. Use low-pile carpets (less than 1.2 inches) with a firm pad beneath.

For wall switch access, place controls no higher than 40 inches from the floor, and consider touch switches near each entrance to halls and rooms. Place electrical outlets 15 inches from the floor.

In the kitchen, the reach for appliances should be comfortable for any seated or standing user. This may mean that instead of using stacked ovens, you would install them side by side at the comfort height of 30 to 36 inches; or creating a recess below work centers, such as cooktops or sinks, to allow for knee space; or providing side access to taller appliances. If you consider the importance of clear sight lines at work counters and storage areas, then you might need to reinstall or rearrange storage items within the universal reach range—15 to 48 inches above the floor.

Similarly, selecting appliances that are user-friendly and intuitive, rather than complicated, benefits all. Are the controls on microwaves, ovens, cooktops, and dishwashers easy to read as well as easy to operate? Does the refrigerator sound an alarm when the door is left open? Are there digital temperature controls on the oven that sound or blink when a limit is reached? Would it help if your microwave or auxiliary oven used numbers and/or pictures to indicate the cooking process?

Hazards in a sink or bathroom area can be averted with built-in controls. Installing faucets that use motion sensors to activate them (and that include a timed, automatic shut-off), or temperature-limiting faucets to prevent scalding, are good examples. For those who are wheelchair-bound, space for a 60-inch turning radius is essential, as are grab bars around tub, shower, shower seat, and toilet.

You can certainly integrate major changes into your house, but just as easily take an approach that is more modification than massive alteration. There are a number of products on the market, both big and small, that can make your life easier and your movement around the house safer. Think of these products as hard-working helping hands that can assist you in many invisible ways. ●

SERVES YOU RIGHT

Having everything at the right height makes microwave cooking from a wheelchair possible, and a pleasure.

OPEN SESAME

Walking into an easy access tub makes safety sense, and helps keep the bather independent.

Space Smarts

NO MATTER THE SIZE OF YOUR ROOMS, THERE is always hidden space you have not yet discovered. Hopefully, as you've read through this book, you have come upon places in your home ready for Right-Sizing—ones that you had not previously considered. Now, change the focus slightly to emphasize living in comfort, which is all about having easy access to whatever you need, daily or frequently.

How high can you comfortably stretch and still safely handle items on shelves above your head? How low would you prefer to bend to get at items below the counter, or on the bottom shelf? Do you feel comfortable on a step stool or crouching to get a much-needed platter or pot?

This reach range is your comfort zone, and it's possible to help yourself by having tools for cooking,

LOWER LEVEL

Placing the microwave at an easy-to-reach height makes it accessible to everyone in the family. Store the accessories below.

RIGHT MOVES

Doing laundry can be challenging if you can't reach the upper cabinets. Install this pull-down insert to overcome this.

bathing, or even laundering come to you instead of you crawling to them. Even the smallest kitchen can make good use of the new generation of innovative cabinet organizers that pull out or pull down.

No space will be wasted when those hard-to-reach shelves above your head are changed to pull-down ones that lower to you. Similarly, there are wall cabinet doors that lift up to reveal the contents.

Plan to make better use of your cabinets. Improve dead corner zones by installing corner base units with mounted shelves that swivel out. Then you don't have to stretch to reach that furthest spot.

The latest trend in kitchen design is clearly leaning toward drawers on base cabinets, instead of doors. New pullout drawers can give you a clear view of what's inside when fully extended. Also, extra-deep or extra-wide drawers create additional space where none previously existed.

These changes are wise investments in universal design for which your knees and aching back will thank you many times over. The even better news is that they don't take up any more space. In fact, the new generation of cabinet inserts actually makes space for you. *That's* a promise worth investigating. ●

Now It's Your Turn

Right-Sizing *Your* Comfort Area

HE LIVING-IN-COMFORT CONCEPT MAKES THE WORKING spaces around your house more easily adaptable to change. These adaptations don't have to wait until you feel older; the aim of universal design is to make your home more efficient and comfortable at whatever age and height you are. Begin the process in the kitchen or bathroom, and no one except the grateful users will be any the wiser. The point is not to turn those rooms into hospital versions, but integrate necessary safe and accessible products for your family's everyday living. ●

Universal Design Products for the Home, in Disguise

THINK EXPANDED AREA FOR WALK-IN SHOWER

Removing a tub/shower and adding a larger shower with a fold-up seat, gives everyone a better bathing experience. Be sure to add a little turn-around space near the shower for easier access for those using a wheelchair.

RESULT:
Allows more space for access, as well as showering

RETHINK MULTITASKING GRAB BARS

Installing grab bars that masquerade as towel bars or a toilet paper holder, make the bathroom safe and secure for all users, especially in a confined area such as a powder room or smaller bath.

RESULT:
More safety created in the same space

THINK FAUCETS FOR SINKS

Lever-handled faucets are easier to use whether your hands are younger or older. The ability to grip the handles, especially when hands are wet, is a bonus that family and friends will enjoy, without realizing the difference.

RESULT:
No change in space, but accessible addition

Resources

This book was planned with you in mind. *I have found that the beautiful pictures are one of the frustrating things about home design books. You spot something really wonderful that would work well in your home, but nothing helps you find the product. Look carefully at the photography credits and the list of manufacturers and retailers that follow. They feature some good-looking products that may find a home in your newly Right-Sized house.*

COMPANY INDEX

Alno Cabinets
617-896-2700
www.alnousa.com

American Leather Furniture
800-456-9599
www.americanleather.com

Arclinea Furniture
415-543-0771
www.arclineasanfrancisco.com

Armstrong Cabinets
800-527-5903
www.armstrong.com

Aristokraft Cabinets
812-482-2527
www.artistokraft.com

Baker Furniture
800-592-2537
www.kohlerinteriors/baker.com

Ballard Designs
800-536-7551
www.ballarddesigns.com

Bassett Furniture
877-525-7070
www.bassettfurniture.com

Bernhardt Furniture
877-442-4321
www.bernhardt.com

Blanco Sinks
800-451-5782
www.blancoamerica.com

Bosch Appliances
800-944-2900
www.bosch-home.com/us

California Closets
888-336-9707
www.californiaclosets.com

Crate&Barrel
214-398-1411
www.crateandbarrel.com

Crossville Ceramics
931-484-2110
www.crossvilleinc.com

Dal Tile
214-398-1411
www.daltile.com

Deca Toilets
877-802-1250
www.deca-us.com

Decora Cabinets
812-482-2527
www.decoracabinets.com

Delta Faucets
800-345-3358
www.deltafaucet.com

Driade
305-572-2900
www.driademiami.com

Duravit Plumbing
888-387-2848
www.duravit.com

Eldorado Stone
800-925-1491
www.eldoradostone.com

Ethan Allen
888-324-3571
www.ethanallen.com

Gerber Plumbing
866-538-5536
www.gerberonline.com

Global Views Accessories
888-956-0030
www.globalviews.com

Great Grabz Grab Bars
866-473-4722
www.greatgrabz.com

Hafele America Hardware
800-423-3931
www.hafele.com

Hammary Furniture
800-443-2920
www.hammary.com

HealthCraft Products
888-629-9992
www.healthcraftproducts.com

Herman Miller Furniture
616-654-3000
www.hermanmiller.com

Hettich Hardware
800-777-1772
www.hettichamerica.com

Hooker Furniture
276-656-3335
www.hookerfurniture.com

Hunter Douglas
800-789-0331
www.hunterdouglas.com

Jacuzzi
800-288-4002
www.jacuzzi.com

Kincaid Furniture
800-438-8207
www.kincaidfurniture.com

Kohler Plumbing
800-456-4537
www.kohler.com

KraftMaid Cabinets
888-562-7744
www.kraftmaid.com

Lane Furniture
877-472-3701
www.lanefurniture.com

Laufen Bath Products
866-696-2493
www.laufen.com

Lea Furniture
336-294-5233
www.leaindustries.com

Lexington Home Brands
336-474-5300
www.lexington.com

Maax Bath Products
888-957-7816
www.maax.com

Martha Stewart Furniture
888-5-MARTHA
www.bernhardt.com/
marthastewartfurniture

Merillat Cabinets
No general number available
www.merillat.com

Miele Appliances
800-999-1360
www.mieleusa.com

Moen
800-289-6636
www.moen.com

MTI Whirlpools
800-783-8827
www.MTIwhirlpools.com

Natuzzi Furniture
800-262-9063
www.natuzzi.com

Omega Cabinets
319-235-5700
www.omegacab.com

Pearl Baths
800-328-2531
www.pearlbaths.com

Perlick Beverage Refrigeration
800-558-5592
www.bringperlickhome.com

Plain & Fancy Custom Cabinetry
800-447-9006
www.plainfancycabinets.com

Poggenpohl Cabinets
800-987-0553
www.poggenpohl-usa.com

Poliform Furniture
888-POLIFORM
www.poliformusa.com

Restoration Hardware
800-910-9845
www.restorationhardware.com

Rev-A-Shelf Cabinet Accessories
800-626-1126
www.rev-a-shelf.com

Riverside Furniture
800-785-8282
www.riverside-furniture.com

Robern Bath Accessories
800-877-2376
www.robern.com

Roca Tile
877-472-3701
www.rocatile.com

Rowe Furniture
800-334-7693
www.rowefurniture.com

Sico Bed Hardware
800-328-6138
www.sicoinc.com

Sidelines Cabinet Hardware
480-767-9091 Ext. 7
www.sidelinesinc.com

Sligh Furniture
616-392-7101
www.sligh.com

Sonia Cabinets
888-766-4387
www.sonia-sa.com

St. Charles Cabinets
662-451-1000
www.stcharlescabinets.com

Stanley Furniture
276-627-2540
www.stanleyfurniture.com

The Container Store
888-266-8246
www.containerstore.com

The Old Wood Company
866-967-9663
www.theoldwoodco.com

Thermador Appliances
800-735-4328
www.thermador.com

Timberlake/American Woodmark
Cabinets/Shenandoah Cabinets
540-665-9100
www.americanwoodmark.com

Universal Furniture
877-804-5535
www.universalfurniture.com

Vanguard Furniture
828-328-5631
www.vanguardfurniture.com

Varenna Kitchens
888-POLIFORM
www.poliformusa.com

Viking Appliances
888-845-4641
www.vikingrange.com

Walker Zanger Tile
818-252-4000 or 732-697-7700
www.walkerzanger.com

Wellborn Cabinets
800-762-4475
www.wellborn.com

Young America Youth Furniture
276-627-2540
www.youngamerica.com

Zoom-Room Hideaway Bed
888-211-1120
www.zoom-room.com

PHOTOGRAPHY CREDITS

(opposite title) Yucatan Wall and Floor Tile
by Laufen available from Roca Tile

4   Ikon Bath Suite from Moen Faucets

CHAPTER ONE — WHAT IS RIGHT-SIZING?
12 Arborcrest Cabinets in Cherry from Armstrong Cabinets
15 (top) Omni Track™ - Craft Room Aplication from Hafele America
    (bottom) Omni Track™ - Laundry Room Application from Hafele America

CHAPTER THREE — WHERE YOU COOK
37 Town & Country Cabinets in Maple from Armstrong Cabinets
39 Arborcrest Cabinets in Cherry from Armstrong Cabinets
40 (top) Masterpiece Marsett Square Cabinets in Maple Pewter with Graphite Glaze from Merillat Cabinets
    (center) Pull-Out Drawer for Pots in Iridescent Blue and Taupe from St. Charles Cabinets
    (bottom) 18-inch Dishwasher from Miele Appliances
42 Stainless Steel Cabinets from St. Charles Cabinets
43 (top) Elfa Walk-In Pantry in White from The Container Store
    (bottom) Camerist Faucet from Moen Faucets
44 Allora Pull-Down Kitchen and Bar/Prep Faucets from Delta Faucet
45 Precis™ Multi-Level Sink with Drainer with Blanco Meridian™ Semi-Professional Faucet in Polished Chrome from Blanco Sinks
46 (top) Backsplash Niche Component Knife Protector from Alno Cabinets
    (bottom) Two-Tier Cookware Storage from Rev-A-Shelf Cabinet Accessories
47 (top) Applause Honeycomb Shades from Hunter Douglas
    (bottom) Kids Zone from Armstrong Cabinets
48 24-inch Gas Range from Viking Range
49 Putnam Cabinets in Maple with Biscotti Finish with Coconut Glaze from KraftMaid Cabinets
50 (top) Kitchen Pantry featuring Walk-in Design in Classic White from California Closets
    (bottom) Shaker Cabinets with Elite Profile in Soft Maple in Dove White Finish from Plain & Fancy Custom Cabinetry
52 Rattan Basket Storage from Sidelines
53 Windham Cabinets in Maple with Wheat Finish from Diamond Cabinets
54 (top) Slim Pantry Pullout in Stainless Steel from St. Charles Cabinets
    (bottom) Induction Cooktop from Thermador
55 (top) Marion Cabinets in Maple with Pearl Finish from Omega Cabinetry
    (bottom) Cargo IQ Wall Cabinet System from Hettich
56 Plus Modo 6 Kitchen from Poggenpohl Cabinets
57 (top left) Bedford Kitchen Island from Ballard Designs
    (top right) Tall Storage in Kitchen in Cotton White from St Charles Cabinets
    (bottom left) Pantos Chef Kitchen from Driade Miami

CHAPTER FOUR — WHERE YOU EAT
59 Dining Table/Chairs from North River Collection from Martha Stewart Furniture™ for Bernhardt Furniture
61 VinoWall™ from Gemstone™ Wall Collection from Eldorado Stone
62 (top) Regency Dining Table #22-400-1, Palladian Bookcase #24-700-1, Sheraton Occasional Chairs #17-432-1 from the Milling Road Collection from Baker Furniture
    (bottom) Victorian Bar/Prep Faucet from Delta Faucet
64 Redin Park Dining Table/Chairs from Bassett Furniture
65 (top) Sunset Key Barstools from Stanley Furniture
    (bottom) Heritage China Base/Sideboard from Country Living Collection from Lane Furniture

RIGHT-SIZING RESOURCES

Here's some good news—you can continue your Right-Sizing even after you have finished reading this book. Below are some book sources that you might find helpful, as well as some websites and associations which should serve as great references.

OTHER BOOKS TO HELP WITH RIGHT-SIZING:

Downsizing Your Home with Style: Living Well in a Smaller Space, by Lauri Ward, Collins Publishing, 2007

Eliminate Chaos: The 10-Step Process to Organize Your Home & Life, by Laura Leist, CPO, CRTS, Sasquatch Books, 2006

Kitchen Design for the 21st Century, – 2nd Edition, by John Drieman and Nancy Elizabeth Hill, Sterling Publishers, 2009

Organize Your Garage in No Time, by Barry J. Izsak, CPO, CRTS, Que Publishing, 2005

Organize Now!: A Week by Week Guide to Simplify Your Space and Your Life, Jennifer Berry, North Light Books, 2008

Store It!: Where to Put all the Things You Need to Keep, by Mervyn Kaufman, Filipacchi Publishing, 2009

The Clutter Diet, by Lorie Marrero, Reason Press, 2009

The Comfortable House, by Mitchell Gold and Bob Williams, Clarkson Potter, 2009

LOOKING FOR ACCESSIBLE DESIGN INFORMATION:

Americans with Disabilities Act (www.ada.gov/stdspdf.htm) This link gives you the standards for accessible design for new construction and remodeling

Center for Universal Design, North Carolina State University (www.design.ncsu.edu/cud/) Information and technical assistance center promoting universal design in homes.

Universal Design Alliance (www.universaldesign.org) Offers advice to homeowners who plan to age in place as well as onsite assessments

LOOKING FOR AGING-IN-PLACE INFORMATION:

National Aging-in-Place Council (www.ageinplace.org) This is a good source for home accessibility consultants and home design service that have been vetted by the National Aging-in-Place Council (NAIPC).

National Association of Home Builders (www.nahb.org) Log on for their directory of Certified Aging-in-Place Specialists (CAPS).

Senior Resource (www.seniorresource.com) Their home assessment checklist is most helpful.

LOOKING FOR KITCHEN AND BATH INFORMATION:

Guide To Kitchen Remodeling (www.guidetokitchenremodeling.com) Their articles are creative and helpful, particularly if this is your first remodel.

National Kitchen and Bath Association (www.nkba.org/consumertools) Provides lists of certified kitchen and bath designers in your area.

Small Bathroom Makeovers (www.smallbathroommakeovers.com) Addresses subjects that are important to consider before taking costly remodeling steps.

LOOKING FOR HELP WITH ORGANIZING INFORMATION:

National Association of Professional Organizers (www.napo.net) Represents 4,200 organizing pros who promise to bring order and efficiency to your home.

National Study Group on Chronic Disorganization (www.nsgcd.org) Makes publication available for the public including a clutter hoarding scale.

Organizing Network (www.organizingnetwork.com) Promises ideas and information, as well as solutions, to help you regain control of your life and home.

Professional Organizers in Canada (www.organizersincanada.com) If you are looking for a Canadian organizer, this resource represents 500 members.

Things In Place (www.thingsinplace.com) Has a handy checklist of "83 Tips for Organizing Your Home" plus a free newsletter, *The 2-Minute Organizer.*

WHERE TO DONATE CLOTHING:

Take time to clean, fold, and organize clothing by size; this will make it easier for the charity to process your contributions. Keep a personal list of items donated if you are taking a tax deduction.

Clothing Donations, Division of Vietnam Veterans of America (www.clothingdonations.org) Picks up household goods as well as clothing. (301-585-4000)

Goodwill Industries (www.goodwill.org) Has 2300 stores around the U.S. Must drop off merchandise. (800-741-0186)

Salvation Army (www.salvationarmy.org) Picks up in many areas and has Family Stores in many communities. (800-728-7825)

Career Gear (www.careergear.org) Provides clothing to low-income men for job interviews in nine locations around U.S. (212-577-6190)

Dress for Success (www.dressforsuccess.org) Supplies clothing to low-income women for job interviews in 75 U.S. cities. (212-532-1922)

Fairy Godmothers Inc. (www.fairygodmothersinc.com) Gives dresses and shoes to needy high school girls for their proms. (215-675-9391); also check with these similar oganizations throughout the U.S.: The Cinderella Project and Glass Slipper Project

Coats for Kids (www.coatsforkids.org) Donates new winter coats to needy children through relationships with retailers such as Target. (703-567-2628)

One Warm Coat (www.onewarmcoat.org) Distributes new and slightly used coats to those in need. (877-663-9275)

Suitcases for Kids (www.suitcasesforkids.org) Gathers luggage for foster children who move from home to home; now in seven states. (No general number.)

WHERE TO DONATE FURNITURE:

Only donate items that are usable, unless directed otherwise. Most nonprofits are not equipped to clean dirty upholstery or repair broken furniture or household items.

Goodwill Industries (see above)

National Furniture Bank Association (www.furniturebanks.org) Provides beds, tables, chairs and other crucial home furnishings to over 100,000 people each year. (877-373-2835)

Purple Heart Foundation (www.moph.org) Accepts furniture in selected locations. (888-414-448)

Salvation Army (see above)

United Way (www.unitedway.org) Searching the United Way website for "furniture" returns a list of fund-raising and other nonprofit opportunities where you can donate your furniture to help your community. (703-836-7112)

OTHER INNOVATIVE RIGHT-SIZING SOURCES:

Pack Rat's Portable Storage (www.packrat.com) Has portable containers that can be delivered to you for temporary storage while Right-Sizing. (800-722-5728)

Port-A-Box Storage (www.portabox.com) Delivers, picks up, and stores storage containers you pack yourself. (888-269-8646)

Portable On Demand Storage (www.pods.com) Delivers, picks up, stores, and/or moves storage container you pack yourself. In U.S. & Canada: (866-229-4120)

Index

About the Author

For ten years **Gale Steves** served as editor-in-chief of *Home* magazine. Under her management, the publication attracted over four million readers nationwide, and established her as an authority on everything to do with the home.

Steves' approach to decorating and remodeling has inspired millions with ideas and real solutions for the home, earning her a reader-friendly reputation along the way.

In 2001, Steves formed Open House Productions, a home industries consulting company, to create an ongoing dialogue between consumers and retailers and manufacturers. It was in response to consumer queries about making their homes more livable that she developed the concept of Right-Sizing. She recognized early on that bigger did not always make better houses, and has been promoting Right-Sizing ever since.

The National Association of Home Builders has recognized Steves' outstanding contribution to the building and remodeling field with a Certificate of Merit. She is listed in *Who's Who of American Women* and was most recently inducted into the YWCA's Academy of Women Achievers.

Steves' consumer magazine experience includes key editorial positions at *Ladies Home Journal, American Home,* and *Woman's Day,* before becoming editor-in-chief of *Woman's Day* Special Interest Publications, a group of 26 lifestyle magazines.

Steves is also the author of several books, including *Weekend Cooking* and *Home Magazine's Best Little Houses.*